The European Empire

'Europe will not be made all at once, or accounting to a single plan'   -- Jean Monnet
founding father of the European Union

'The European Union is, as it has been, not a super-state... At the same time, we are not either an international organization... We are what some authors call the first 'non-imperial empire"
-- Jose-M. Durão Barroso
ex-President of the European Commission

The EU has 'produced a degree of unity that had not been seen in Europe since the Holy Roman Empire'   -- Henry Kissinger
ex-Secretary of State of the United States

'The states have limited their sovereign rights, albeit within limited fields, and have thus created a body of law which binds both their nationals and themselves'   - European Court of Justice

'The Commission shall be completely independent and the members of the Commission shall neither seek nor take instructions from any Government or other institutions, body, office or entity'

-- Treaty on European Union

'We want a European Union that is bigger and more ambitious on big things, and smaller and more modest on small things'

-- Jean-Claude Juncker
President of the European Commission

'The euro is irreversible' and the European Central Bank is 'ready to do whatever it takes to preserve the euro'   -- Mario Draghi
President of the European Central Bank

'A united Europe, with a reunited Germany at its cente not a German Europe, but a European Germany'   -- Thomas Mann
German writer, Nobel Prize in Literature laureate

'Russia is our strategic problem'   -- Donald Tusk
President of the European Council

'We have an imperative to handle the EU's borders, as we all know from the Roman empire, big empires go down if the borders are not well protected'   – Mark Rutte

President of the Council of the EU

'The political divide is not left and right anymore, but globalists and patriots...as in neither in Greece or Spain there is no equivalent to the National Fron, it is the extreme left that takes our place'
                                         – Marine Le Pen

leader of the National Front of France

'I'm not sure we would manage a Grexit, because managing the collapse of a monetary union takes a great deal of expertise, and I'm not sure we have it here in Greece without the help of outsiders'
                                        – Yanis Varoufakis

ex-minister of finances of Greece

'Having the UK in the EU gives us much greater confidence about the strength of the transatlantic union... We want to make sure that the United Kingdom continues to have that influence'
                                       -- Barack Obama

President of the United States

The European Empire

Also by Josep Colomer

The Science of Politics. An Introduction
(Oxford University Press)

How Global Institutions Rule the World
(Palgrave-Macmillan)

Great Empires, Small Nations.
The uncertain future of the sovereign state
(Routledge)

Comparative European Politics (editor)
(Routledge, 3rd edition)

Personal website:
www.josepcolomer.com

The European Empire

Josep M. Colomer

Winner of the
Fondation Europa Cultural
Essay Prize
2016

Available for purchase at www.amazon.com
and amazon.co.uk

ISBN 10: 1523318902
ISBN 13: 9781523318902
Library of Congress LCCN

CONTENTS

Introduction:
The Endurable Incompleteness of Europe 1

1. Is the European Union an Empire? 7

2. Goodbye, Sovereignty 23

3. The German Core 36

4. The Wild East 48

5. What Has Europe Done for Us? 66

6. Multiple Speeds 81

7. Too Much Regulation, Too Little Budget 91

8. A Faustian Bargain 104

9. The Brussels Consensus 113

10. The Rule of Experts 130

11. Nationalist Resistances 147

12. To Brexit or Not to Brexit 167

Conclusion: **The Unsettled Future of the European Union** 187

Acknowledgments and Sources 194

The Endurable Incompleteness of Europe

The European Union (EU) has recently been under siege from the West, from the East and from the South, in this order of importance. On the West, Brexit, that is, the departure of Great Britain from the Union, could shake the entire project of a united Europe. On the East, frontier struggles with the Russian empire, including especially in Ukraine, and massive immigrations from the Middle East, test the viability of a Union without clear, fixed borders. In the South, the Greek crisis has shown the vulnerability of peripheral countries that have not caught up, but have rather widened their gap with the central core around Germany. Some people bet that the European Union will not be able to survive this type of crises and will collapse in a non-remote future. The resilience of the United States and the emergence of new economies, especially in Asia, also sketch an image of European decline.

However, even during the most recent Great Recession, the number of member states of the European Union has increased, as have the number of countries using the common currency. The commercial and monetary union of most of Europe has recently been followed by fiscal and banking unions. Every year, a few dozen new EU regulations become directly binding on all European citizens. Up to half of new national legislation enacted in most countries derives from the EU. In order to promote economic recovery, the European Commission has taken the initiative to launch investments in infrastructure. The European Central Bank is much more active than was expected just a few years ago. The Brussels and Frankfurt policy consensus is broadly accepted all across the continent. Hundreds of thousands of people, especially from Africa and the Middle East, are attracted by the European way of life and try to migrate or seek refuge in Europe.

It is possible to comprehend both the challenges and the achievements of the European Union just sketched above in a new light. The turnabouts of the EU are typical of an "empire". This type of political organization lies somewhere in between the international organization and the state. Its main distinctive characteristic is to be united in diversity –precisely the motto of the European Union--, which implies numerous asymmetries in the links among its members.

On the one hand, the EU is much more than an international diplomatic organization of sovereign states. In fact, the Union has pooled many of the traditional powers of the states, which keep holding their sovereignty only as an outdated juridical reference. But, on the other hand, the EU is also much less than a super-state or a complete federation. It has no stable borders, different countries have different degrees of commitment to certain common policies, and some, as mentioned at the beginning, may consider exit. There is no such as thing as a United States of Europe in the observable horizon. Even less a European super-state.

Rather than as an international organization, a state or a federation, the European Union can be understood, thus, as an "empire". Most of the history of the world has involved a succession of empires. But the notion of empire has been neglected in recent times due to the prevalence of the modern form of political organization based on the "state", especially in Europe. The European Union is nowadays a highly asymmetric, inward-looking, non-colonialist empire. It can survive and thrive precisely because it is characteristic of empires to have uneven levels of formal integration and diverse degrees of people's allegiance to the center. Empires also expand and contract, as may happen to the EU.

This essay bets on this future. Within the European Union, territorial, economic, and institutional asymmetries will last. Tensions between pulls for more integration and nationalist resistances will persist. Some provisional borders of the Union will prove to be fragile and vulnerable. New entrances and new exits may occur. But strong elements of union of the continent will remain and may be deepened. Europe will not become, again, the stage for permanent rivalries and battles between well bordered, allegedly sovereign states.

The European empire is just one egregious case of the processes of increasing interdependence among countries that can be observed all over the world. Transnational trade, multinational companies and trans-border investments, massive migrations, frequent and long-distance travels, and worldwide networks of communications have changed the planet in the last few decades. The traditional form of political organization based on the state is increasingly unfit for such a world. The mismatch is particularly notorious in Europe. On the one hand, the levels of economic activity and interdependence among European countries are particularly high. On the other hand, as the modern form of state was invented in Europe, some European states still show their grasping tentacles and their arrogant ambition of exclusivity.

New political and institutional formulas are needed to deal efficiently with an interdependent world. In Europe, the "imperial" form of internal political organization can be successful because it can respond with flexibility to such unavoidable challenge.

1

Is the European Union an Empire?

The British Prime Minister was the president of turn of the Council of the European Union for six months. He was coming from the summit meeting of prime ministers and presidents, rather frustrated by its ineffectiveness, and exclaimed to his special advisor:

> "Being President of Europe is not enough! Europe is an empire; it needs an Emperor!"

A few minutes later, back in his office, the Cabinet Secretary clarified to the Prime Minister a likely source of his distress:

"Prime Minister" –he said with distinctive, sophisticated boldness--, "what it boils down to, as far as you are concerned, is the difference between years of being ahead of an Empire of nearly 500 million people and chairing the Council of Ministers of the European Union for six months!"

This was a fictional exchange in the amusing BBC's TV series *Yes, Prime Minister*, written by Antony Jay and Jonathan Lynn, as revived in 2013. Yet, even if fictional, the dialog is insightful about the real European Union and it highlights a few crucial points that merit discussion. They include the following:

First, it is difficult to govern Europe effectively with the currently existing, not very much centralized institutions. Second, the United Kingdom is wary of the European Union because it was used to ruling its own large empire and now it's only one more member of another empire. And third and, above all, the European Union is an empire.

A non-imperialistic empire

That the European Union can be understood as an empire is a point that has been raised not only as a political satire. It is also a serious elaboration both by scholars who thoroughly study and analyze this interesting type of political beast and by actual top officers of the Union. To the untrained ear, "Empire" may sound like implying authoritarianism and violent conquest. But, of course, this is not the case. Empire means a form of political organization for a vast territory which is based on a variety of formulas to link the units to the center, and, as not having fixed borders it is also open to changes in its membership.

One of the most celebrated occasions to popularize the idea of Europe as an empire was a long, largely improvised declaration by the president of the European Commission, Jose M. Durão Barroso, in 2007. At a massively attended press conference in the European Parliament in Strasbourg, Barroso defined the European Union as "a non-imperial empire". The occasion was the announcement of a "Reform Treaty", eventually called the "Treaty of Lisbon," which is currently enforced as a kind of constitutional-type rules of the European Union.

In front of such a great challenge, a Dutch journalist (whose name is not recorded) asked how the European Union as an innovative political entity could be defined. The journalist wondered: "Europe will not become a super-state, but it's also not an international organization or a playground for diplomats. What will the European Union be when the new treaty will be launched?"

The President of the European Commission responded:

> "The European Union is, as it has been, not a super-state, as you said. We are not the United States of Europe in the way we have the United States of America; we are not. At the same time, we are not either an international organization like NATO [North Atlantic Treaty Organization] or OECD [Organization for Economic Cooperation and Development] or the Council of Europe or whatever. We are, in fact, a very special construction, unique... Some people said that we are an Unidentified Political Object; it's a distinct definition, and I think we should not

be depressed with that, it's in a way a very successful experiment."

Then, Barroso launched his main point:

"Sometimes I like to compare the European Union as a creation to the organization of empires. Empires! Because we have the dimension of empires. But there is a great difference. The empires were usually made through force, with a center that was imposing a diktat, a will, on the others. And now we are what some authors call the first 'non-imperial empire'. We have, by dimension, 27 countries that freely decided to work together to pool their sovereignties (if you want to use that concept of sovereignty) and work together... I believe it's a great construction, and we should be proud of it. At least we in the Commission are proud of what we are."

When Jose M. Durão Barroso said that the European Union could be conceived as a "non-imperial empire", he was alluding to the difference between an imperialistic policy and an imperial polity. This distinction needs to be clarified.

Certainly the EU's foreign policy --to the extent that such a thing exists-- is not imperialistic in the classical sense of conquest and domination of foreign lands and populations. The EU does not pretend to build any empire like the old Spanish, British, French or other transcontinental colonial empires. The EU doesn't practice either an imperialistic policy aiming at absorbing European territories by force, as was the case of Napoleon's or Hitler's attempted --and very short-lived-- continental European empires.

What "empire" means, in this case, is not a foreign policy, but a form of polity, that is, a form of organization of a political community. A polity can be organized as a city, a county, a region, a state, a federation, or an international organization, among other categories, each based on different scales of the territories under their jurisdictions. The specific form of polity called "empire" implies a large area and it's different from both a sovereign state, which tends to be smaller, and a great international organization formed by sovereign states. The EU is, on the one hand, far more than an international organization such as NATO or others mentioned in the exchange reproduced above. But, on the other hand, it is much less than a very large, super state or federation.

An imperialistic policy is something different. In fact, it can be implemented not only by an empire, but also by the other forms of polity. There can be imperialistic states, as was the case, just mentioned, of the colonial empires of European states in America, Africa, and Asia. And there can even be imperialistic cities, as historical experiences such as those of Sparta or Venice, for instance, can suggest. Likewise, polities like a city, a state or an empire can do non-imperialistic policies, but favor transnational cooperation and peaceful coexistence. The modern history of Europe shows all these alternatives. So an imperialistic policy and an imperial polity are two different things that may come together or not.

The medieval European Empire

Some of the academic "authors" to whom Barroso was alluding to we have suggested a historical analogy between the current European Union and the medieval Holy Roman and German Empire (see 'Sources' at the end of the book). In this perspective, the European Union may not be a "unique" experience of non-imperial empire, as there have been other political organizations of that sort in the history of mankind.

Regarding the medieval experience, one would say that the current European empire looks more German than Roman, if the usual semi-humorous cliché can be accepted. But the analogy is suggestive enough in many respects, as both the medieval Empire and the current Union have movable borders, common and pegged currencies, varied representative institutions, and they both give prevalence to negotiations and to other peaceful and legalistic means of resolving conflicts. None of them is "imperialistic" in the sense of a policy of conquest.

Depending on how one dates it, the Holy Roman and German Empire lasted about one thousand years: from the initial gathering of central European lands by the Frankish King Charlemagne, who was crowned emperor in 800, to its dissolution at Napoleon's imperative in 1806. In contrast to the ancient Roman Empire, the medieval Holy Roman Empire didn't annex territories on the basis of military occupation, but by consensual enlargements of the initial core. In a rather loose union, the Empire contained up to more 300 fiefs and more than 80 cities, including a number of republics that proclaimed themselves "free", that is, self-governed, precisely because they accepted the authority of the Emperor. The borders of the Holy Roman Empire were open and flexible until mid-fourteenth century. In spite of this, the Empire successfully resisted repeated invasions by the neighbor and rival Ottoman Empire for a few centuries.

Like in the current Union, there was a form of common monetary system in medieval Europe. The currencies used in different parts of the Holy Roman Empire were accepted for trade based on the value of the metal of their coins or they were pegged in value to each other, which greatly facilitated cross-European trade. The principalities and cities retained the right to mint their own coins, usually with the imperial eagle on one side and the local coat of arms on the other, which may also sound familiar nowadays to people living in the Euro-zone.

The form of government of the Empire was based on delegates from the member units. The Imperial Diet or assembly was in permanent session from the mid-seventeenth century on. The Diet worked by negotiating agreements and compromises, especially on the allocation of powers and the payments of debts, which sometimes were solved by giving weighted votes to their members for reference to their population or size. Does this also sound familiar?

Periodically, a College of between seven and ten representatives of the major principalities and other units elected the Emperor, more formally when the territorial limits of the Empire became more stable; that is from the fourteenth century on. This was in contrast to the formation of dynasties and the succession by primogeniture, which were novelties introduced by absolutist monarchs. The latter were precisely the usual rivals that resisted the Emperor's powers and tried to build sovereign states.

Some important features of the Holy Roman and German Empire that can evoke some of the current European Union ones include, thus: movable frontiers for a very long period until relatively more stable borders were fixed, pegged currencies and broad trade, rule by a permanent body formed by representatives of the territorial units with votes weighted by their size, decisions made by broad negotiations and compromises, as well as overlapping authorities and diverse institutional formulas across Europe –that is, strong links of unity together with remarkable religious, language and cultural diversity.

The similarities between the current European endeavor and the medieval experience have been acknowledged even by the most egregious defender of the international "order" based on sovereign states' permanent rivalries and wars. According to Henry Kissinger, the current Union is "more like the Holy Roman Empire than the Europe of the nineteenth century"; the current institutionalization of the European Union has "produced a degree of unity that had not been seen in Europe since the Holy Roman Empire".

An empire is not a federation

It's interesting that Jose M. Durão Barroso, in his largely improvised speech above quoted, in which he remarked that the European Union is neither a super state nor an international organization, also felt the need to affirm that it is not a federation either. That is, the EU is not the United States of Europe in the same way as we have the United States of America.

Actually, notorious proposals to build the United States of Europe were raised in the aftermath of the catastrophic World War II, which has been considered a kind of European civil war. One of the earliest ones was presented by the French activist Jean Monnet, who would be a main inspirer of the first plans for economic cooperation among France, Germany and other European states. Still during the war, he anticipated:

> "There will be no peace in Europe if the states rebuild themselves on the basis of national sovereignty... The countries of Europe are not strong enough individually to be able to

guarantee prosperity and social development for their peoples. The states of Europe must, therefore, form a federation or a European entity that would make them into a common economic unit."

On the other side of the channel, British Prime Minister, Winston Churchill, also advised continental Europeans to unite themselves, while Britain would remain outside (as long as it could maintain its own empire).

"If the European countries succeed in uniting –he said--, their three to four hundred million inhabitants would know, by the fruit of their common heritage, a prosperity, a glory, a happiness that no boundary, no border could contain... We must construct such a thing as the United States of Europe".

And on the other side of the ocean, former supreme commander of the Allied Forces in Europe during World War II and President of the United States, Dwight Eisenhower, also warned: "I believe there is no real answer to the European problem until there is definitely established a United States of Europe".

To place these proposals in a realistic context, we should be aware that the USA, as we know it today, was not created when independence was achieved and an innovative constitution was approved by the late eighteenth century. The American Union was built through a very long process of increasing centralization of powers pooled from previously existing states and imposed on newly annexed territories. It involved one of the most lethal Civil Wars ever, one that was fought between those favoring the consolidation of the federation and those resisting such a project by claiming the "sovereignty" of the states, in the 1860s. Before the Civil War, most Americans still spoke of the United States in the plural: the United States "are"; only gradually in the period of Reconstruction after the Civil War, by the late nineteenth century, the United States began to be referred to in the singular: the United States "is".

Building the United States of America required the establishment of regular democratic institutions in all the states, as well as the creation of new federal institutions in Washington. In fact, the process lasted for near 140 years. It started with the declaration of independence in 1776. But it was completed only with the creation of the Federal Reserve and the Federal Bureau of Investigation, among other important federal institutions, and the homogenization of the rules to elect the House of Representatives, the Senate and the Presidential Electoral College in all the states from about 1911-1914.

Jean Monnet envisaged a future politically united Europe as "a sort of second America". Until the present moment, the process of building the European Union has lasted for less than half the time the American experience needed to reach its completion. But about sixty years after the foundational Treaty of Rome, it's pretty clear that in spite of the predictions, advice, warnings and hopes above quoted, the United States of Europe, conceived as a democratic, solidly institutionalized and well-established federation, more or less like the United States of America, is not something visible on the foreseeable horizon. This observation may disappoint enthusiasts of federalism. But it should also disband euroskeptics' worries and fears of a new all-powerful center able to rule all over Europe by decree.

Like a federation, the European Union has dissolved the absolute sovereignties of the states into a set of multiple levels of government focused on policy issues at different territorial scales. But unlike a federation, the European Union has no fixed borders, it involves different commitments of state members with the different common policies, and it's organized with mixed institutional formulas at the central level. The most distinctive characteristic of the European empire is its asymmetries, whether regarding the territory, the economy, the powers of the states, and the institutions.

2

Goodbye, Sovereignty

The concept of sovereignty was invented in Europe and in Europe is dying. The history of most civilizations typically involves a series of rising and falling empires with a variety of internal formulas. But in Europe the medieval Empire, which we reviewed in the previous chapter, was replaced with multiple states, each trying to affirm its internal compactness and its external independence.

It has been characteristic of the rulers of modern states to assert their sovereignty against the others and to use the notions of the "raison d'état" and "national interest", especially since these concepts got adherence after the Treaty of Westphalia in the seventeenth century. With the help of theoreticians like the English Thomas Hobbes and the French Jean Bodin, certain attributes that the absolute monarchs had claimed for themselves were transferred to "the state". Sovereignty was conceived as an "absolute, perpetual, inalienable, and indivisible" power, the supreme source of authority within clearly-defined borders. But the fight for borders and transcontinental colonial empires led the states to permanent rivalries and increasingly bloody wars.

After the Second World War, the rulers of the European states, especially France and Germany, decided to try to build a kind of internal empire among them, that is, on European soil, in order to promote economic cooperation and the resolution of conflicts by peaceful means. That was the beginning of the end of the sovereignty of the states and the beginning of a new process to build, again, a broad union of Europe.

The traditional model of the sovereign national state pretended that one size and one institutional regime fit all. Each state aimed at establishing rigid control of the territory, concentration of power, hierarchical institutional structure, and nationalistic homogenization. As in the Greek myth of Procustus, those not fitting the one-size bed were amputated at the legs. But in the current Europe and the interdependent and complex world, multiple sizes are needed for the provision of a diversity of public goods. A single sovereignty is not efficient almost anywhere anymore.

Multiple levels of government

Some academic authors have converged on interpreting the European Union as a case of "multilevel" governance. This means that each of the multiple levels of government that currently exist, from city and region to state and Europe, has powers to make decisions on different issues. The notion of multi-level governance is incompatible with the classical notion of sovereignty. It makes sense, in contrast, in the context of a pluralistic, complex Empire.

Dividing powers among different levels of government is more efficient than the typical centralization in large unitary states. It's clear that certain public goods are better provided at very large scales. They include, for example, defense, security and protection from terrorism, trade rules and currency, regulation of transnational finances, energy, broad transport routes and communication networks, immigration, research and access to scientific and artistic works. It's a question of efficiency costs: the larger the scale at which these goods and services can be provided, the better for all.

In contrast, other provisions may fit midsize territorial ranges such as those of some existing states, including roads and highways, the management of the waters of river basins, or the administration of civil law and justice. In turn, regional governments can focus on urban planning and public works, local commerce, as well as the management of religious, racial or language differences. Local governments can efficiently supply services such as parks, schools and hospitals, libraries and museums, or garbage removal.

In a structure of power at multiple levels like this, no single level of government has the monopoly of legitimacy and coercion. This kind of "vertical" division of powers, from the city to the

Union, implies that each level of government can have the power to make final decisions on some issues. But none of the levels of government has complete sovereignty to make final decisions on all the issues submitted to public consideration.

The criterion of "subsidiarity", as formally adopted by the EU, allocates the issues to the lowest level at which they can be efficiently provided. So better to provide public goods and services at the local level than at state level, and better by the state than by the Union. But on the issues under its jurisdiction, European Union law has priority over state law. Even if the states may keep statements of "legal" sovereignty. But the "material" sovereignty —as is put by constitutional lawyers—is divided, and --as sovereignty is, by definition, indivisible-- it has vanished as such.

In fact, "sovereignty" has become one of the most obsolete political concepts in the current world, and especially in Europe. The notion of sovereignty implies a centralized monopoly of power. But in the typical imperial form of government that fits the current European Union, no local, state or imperial government asserts itself as fully sovereign in front the others. The member-states of the European Union have pooled their previously affirmed sovereignties, but they have not created a new European sovereignty.

Not even constitutional sovereignty

Most of the current member-states of the European Union don't even place the notion of state or national sovereignty at the center of their constitutional order any more. Allow me to demonstrate using the 28 member-states constitutional texts currently enforced.

First, the laws, statutes, court sentences, treaties and other sources that make up the political regime of the United Kingdom enshrine only the principle of "parliamentary sovereignty", which has been made compatible with following EU law and complying with international standards. In the written constitutions of another ten EU member states, the word "sovereignty" is not even mentioned (Austria, Belgium, Cyprus, Czech Republic, Denmark, Germany, Italy, Luxembourg, Netherlands, Sweden). In the current French constitution, rhetorical references are made to the principles of the Revolution placing sovereignty in "the people". Similar expressions are used only as plain synonym of democracy in the constitutions of six more countries (Estonia, Finland, Greece, Hungary, Latvia, Portugal). As an extreme case, Slovenia's candidacy to EU's membership moved its constitution-makers to mention explicitly, no less than eight times, that the republic would "transfer the exercise of sovereign rights to international organizations".

In contrast, the sovereignty of the "state" is affirmed in only four countries (the recently decolonized islands of Ireland and Malta and the historically threatened Poland and Slovakia). The sovereignty of the "nation" appears only in the constitutions of four republics recently liberated from imperial Soviet control (Bulgaria, Croatia, Lithuania, and Romania). As an extreme case, "national sovereignty" appears in the constitution of highly nationalistic Spain, which also assigns its defense to the Armed Forces.

Firing the Coach

Some political consequences of the vanishing of the sovereignty of the states in the context of an increasingly effective European Union were cleverly remarked by the current President of the European Commission, Jean-Claude Juncker. This was when he was President of the finance ministers of the Euro-zone in charge of crafting, implementing and overseeing Europe-wide economic policies and, at the same time, Prime Minister of Luxembourg. Juncker was aware of the mismatch between the two jobs when he confessed: "We all know what to do, but we don't know how to get re-elected once we will have done it."

Actually, Juncker eventually solved his problem by quitting Luxembourg politics and running for a seat in the European Parliament and the presidency of the Commission, the offices that better fit his policy concerns. From there he can focus on demands and expectations at the European level and not to have to worry much about anticipating reactions from voters and taxpayers in Luxembourg.

But for many politicians in Europe, the mismatch between Europe-wide policy and domestic politics persists. In many countries, many public decisions are heavily dependent on the European Union. Most public spending is driven by EU directives and by previously committed obligations including public servant salaries, social security and healthcare, debt interests, and other financial transfers and expenses. Also, most discretionary spending is constrained by long-term programs and a moderate continuity. It can be estimated that, in most countries, a complete change of parties in government permits changing the allocation of expenditures for a maximum value of about 4% of GDP. As multiparty coalitions also limit policy change, in practice the actual reallocation of resources from one election to another is even lower.

Some consequences of the shift of power to the EU on the downgrading of domestic politics are highly visible. They include the un-fulfillment of traditional party platforms, especially regarding the management of macro-economic issues, and the subsequent banalization of political campaigning. Many political procedures and rituals at the state level are still developed as if the state kept full sovereign control on all major policy decisions. However, the relation between the degradation of the classical political show, the increasing volatility of votes, parties and governments, and the Europeanization and internationalization of public affairs has not always been remarked.

As a consequence of loss of sovereignty and externally induced policy stability, many politicians competing under belligerent partisan labels disappoint their electoral promises and don't know much how to get re-elected. In fact, since the beginning of the Great Recession in 2008, political parties in government have been losing elections with higher frequency than ever before. Outstanding episodes include the following. In the United Kingdom in 2010, the incumbent Labour Party obtained its worst result in proportion of votes since the First World War, when it became a government party for the first time. In Hungary in 2010, the Social-democrats in government lost more than half of their previous electoral support. In Ireland in 2011, the Fianna Fail, the most common ruling party since the country's independence, slipped to third in votes. In Spain in 2011, the incumbent Socialists got their worst result since the reestablishment of democracy in the 1970s. In Slovenia in 2011, the incumbent Social-democrats lost two-thirds of their previous votes. In France in 2012, the incumbent Conservative President was the first not to be reelected in more than thirty years. In Bulgaria in 2013, the incumbent Conservatives lost one-fourth of their previous support and were replaced by a government led by an independent and formed by both nonpartisan experts and a coalition of parties. In the Czech Republic in 2013 the incumbent three-party center-right coalition lost almost half of its previous support while other three parties obtained higher numbers of votes than any of them. In Greece in 2012, the incumbent Socialists lost more than two-thirds of their previous support and became third in votes. A new election had to be called six weeks later to try to produce an alternative multiparty majority. But in the following election, in 2015, the incumbent New Democracy party obtained its worst result ever in terms of seats, and its government partner, the Socialists, descended to seventh place, which was basically confirmed in a new snap election a few months later.

Looking to the first two elections in each member state of the EU since 2008, we see that, on average, the incumbent prime minister's or president's party has lost about one-fifth of the voting support obtained in the immediately previous election (about three times a higher relative loss than in the elections in the previous decade). Also, in near two-thirds of the elections the incumbent prime minister's or president's party has been replaced by an opposition party (in contrast to less than one-third in previous decades).

The voters' electoral behavior in many countries during the recent Great Recession has been similar to the usual reaction to "firing the coach" in sports when a team underperforms regarding previous achievements and usual expectations. In football and other team sports, firing the coach tends to be a ritual scapegoating. Sport club members, like voters in our case, can be aware of the fact that a failure, such a team's or an economy's underperformance, is due to a number of factors that cannot be fairly simplified as only bad management --such as the European and global interdependence of most domestic economies. But managers and governments are punished, even if many people realize that they are not always fully responsible for all the team's or the economy's performance, precisely because after being disappointed in their expectations, voters cannot trust the same people's promises for the future anymore.

Two outstanding exceptions to the electoral trends above mentioned include Germany and the United Kingdom, where the incumbent Prime minister's parties, the Christian-democrats led by Angela Merkel and the Conservatives led by David Cameron, respectively, were successfully re-elected in 2013 and 2015. In today's Europe, they both appear as leading effective, but alternative ways of dealing with economic problems. Their success may also help explain their different approaches to the development of the European Union.

3

The German Core

In the aftermath of World War II, when the specter of Nazism was still haunting Europe, the German novelist Thomas Mann envisioned". But he warned about the difficulties that were going to be created by the "fear by other peoples of Germany and hegemonic plans". He called "not for a German Europe, but for a European Germany." In a kind of response, the newly elected Chancellor Konrad Adenauer solemnly proclaimed: "German problems can only be solved under a European roof".

When, more than forty years later, Germany reunified and became the most populated country and the largest economy of the European Union, some observers raised, again, the fear of German dominance. Most preferences were, of course, for a European Germany. Having Germany within the European Union was a guarantee of peace. And, indeed, in spite of some appearances, Germany is not the "hegemon" of the European Union. A hegemonic country would be one that would able to dominate and control all the other countries within its sphere of influence by political, economic or military means. In the historical experience of Europe, the fight for hegemony has always conduced to war.

Nowadays, Germany is at the "core" of the European Union. But a core is formed by well-integrated countries that cooperate among themselves and enable smaller, willing groups of member states to forge ahead. An empire can be pluralistic and internally balanced, especially if it works by consensus as the EU does, without relying upon a hegemonic power. In Europe, Germany does not dominate, but it rather leads by example, especially on economic and integration matters. But the European Union has also adopted and developed a political model of decision-making by consensus that it's typical of the German democratic experience. And —in case it must be reminded-- the most widely used language in the EU's institutions is not German, but English, followed by French.

Moved to the center

Germany is currently located in a rather central position within the EU's territory. Its central location is the result of a long process of successive enlargements of the EU all azimuths, which has moved the center from France to Germany and has more clearly created the Southern and Eastern peripheries.

From its six initial members, the European Community (EC) has expanded towards the West, the South, the North, and the East. The initial axis, which was formed by the traditional enemies in a series of European wars: France and Germany, immediately attracted the intermediately located, traditional first victims of the two great powers' invasions: Belgium, the Netherlands, and Luxembourg. They were also joined by Italy, which was the host of the signature of the foundational treaty of Rome. At that time, the population of Germany was nearly half of the total population of the EC (47 percent, to be precise). The German Gross Domestic Product (GDP) was about 40 percent of the European Community's GDP.

Yet, the European Community institutions were headquartered away from Germany: in Brussels, Strasbourg, and Luxembourg. Germany was clamorously absent from top European institutional offices for several decades. The presidents of the early three Communities on Coal and Steel, Atomic Energy, and the Economy in the 1950s and 1960s were six Frenchmen, two Italians, and only one German. The next eleven presidents of the unified European Commission since 1967 have been recruited from each of the other five initial member-states plus the United Kingdom and Portugal, but none from Germany.

The first of the enlargements of the European Community was mostly westward, towards the Atlantic Ocean. The United Kingdom, Ireland and Denmark joined the EC in the 1970s. The Belgians and the Dutch had worked hard to have the Britons in the EC. They expected that a more balanced configuration with three great partners would lighten pressure in comparison with being in a sandwich between the usual two big neighbors.

The second enlargement of the Community was southwards, towards the Mediterranean Sea. It incorporated three countries that had recently replaced military dictatorships with democratic regimes: Greece, Portugal, and Spain. For these countries, membership to the European institutions was a synonym of guaranteed freedom. Especially for Spain, which also joined the NATO in the process, it also meant leaving a long-lasting international relegation.

Major changes, now more around Germany, began to be introduced after the fall of the Berlin Wall, the dissolution of the Soviet Union, the end of the Cold War, and the re-foundation of the European Union in the 1990s. First, the Western Federal Republic of Germany annexed the Eastern, former Communist-dominated lands. A few years later, the European Central Bank was designed on the model of the Bundesbank, that is, with priority to its independence and a mandate to contain the perils of inflation. For the first time, a high office of the EU was headquartered in

Germany, in Frankfurt am Main, with the intention to keep it more independent from the other EU's institutions located in Brussels.

A succession of post-Cold War enlargements ensued. They included, first, the countries that had remained neutral between the Western and the Soviet blocks and outside the corresponding military alliances: Austria, Finland, and Sweden. Then, in a few waves, three former members of the Soviet Union: Estonia, Latvia, and Lithuania; six former members of the Soviet-dominated military Warsaw Pact and the economic Council for Mutual Economic Assistance (Comecon): Bulgaria, Czech Republic, Hungary, Poland, Romania, and Slovakia; two former members of communist Yugoslavia: Slovenia and Croatia; as well as two former British colonies in small Mediterranean islands: Cyprus and Malta.

After these enlargements all azimuths –West, South, North, and East--, Germany found itself located around the geographic center of the EU territory. If you draw an X over the current map of the European Union with vanes from Scotland to Southeast Bulgaria and from East Finland to

Gibraltar, the crossing point lies almost exactly on Berlin.

A European Germany

Yet through the successive enlargements, the relative size and importance of Germany within the Union –as that of France or any other old member-- has greatly decreased. The population of Germany is currently only one-sixth of the total population of the Union, while it was three times relatively higher at the foundational moment of the EC, as mentioned. The German GDP is only one-fifth of the total GDP of the Union, that is, it has half the relative weight of sixty years ago. The German economy is also highly integrated in Europe, especially in terms of trade, investments, and loans.

The relative sizes of the member-states were reflected for a long while in the distribution of weighted votes in the Council of the European Union. They are now the basis for the apportionment of seats in the European Parliament, as well as for each country's contributions to the EU's budget and the funds of the European Central Bank. These wide distributions of votes, finances, and power among member states make collective decisions feasible not by means of any "hegemon", but only on the basis of very broad negotiations and agreements.

Germany' capability to become a great power in the global scene is considerably marred by its people's and leaders' reluctance to engage more in international affairs. German foreign policy greatly deals with the contended Eastern borders of the EU. Beyond that, ambitious diplomatic initiatives lack the support of effective military resources. After World War II, the German government was not recognized defense powers. After the reunification, most units were disbanded or transferred to a multinational corps in NATO. Nowadays, the German army is one of the lowest budgeted ones in the world in terms of share of GDP and only the 30th military force in the world in absolute terms of active troops.

In Europe, only the United Kingdom and France have nuclear weapons and operational armies with a global orientation. The United Kingdom keeps playing a vital role of transatlantic bridge between Europe and the United States, in spite of recent cuts in the British military budget. In the NATO Council, all state members have an equally weighted voice and decisions are made on the basis of common accords. In the Group of Seven (G-7), which is the closest thing to a world government that has ever existed, Germany sits together with three more European members: the United Kingdom, France and Italy, as well as the presidents of the European Commission and of the European Council. And the G-7 also makes decisions by consensus.

The German model

Actually, Germany had already begun to become European from the very moment it lost the War, was occupied by the Allies, and was imposed a constraining constitution (which was not even named as such) meant to prevent new authoritarian experiments. Only the occupying Soviets desired a strong, unified government, which they eventually established in their Eastern part. In the West, by contrast, priority was given to limiting the powers of the German state. In the words of the United States Secretary of State at the time, a strong state was not desirable because "it could be too readily converted to the domination of a regime similar to the Nazis". As it was put by the British Foreign minister, "all powers should be vested in the lands except such as are expressly delegated to the central government". His French colleague went so far as to conceive of the national parliament as a chamber of mere "coordination" of lands.

Germany was able to reunify only because it had become a full-fledged, committed member of the European Community and NATO. Direct negotiations between the West Federal Republic and the East Democratic Republic over the Berlin Wall were inconceivable during the Cold War. Germany needed to be European to be able to be Germany again. Once reunified, Germany found itself at the core of Europe and has since kept pressing forward with integration.

Not in spite of, but thanks to its initial constitutional restrictions, the federal democratic regime of Germany has developed a consensual and very effective model of decision-making. In the lower chamber of parliament, a moderate multi-party system has supported a series of coalition cabinets in four different two-party combinations involving the Christian-democrats and their permanent partners the Bavarian Social-Christians, the Social-democrats, the Free-democrats, and the Greens. At the same time, the upper chamber has become the setting for inter-territorial cooperation among the Laender, for broadening the political support to legislative and governmental decision-making, and for selecting high officers of the judiciary, the central bank and other independent bodies of experts. More specifically, during most of the time since 2005, including the recent Great Recession, Germany has been governed by "grand coalition" cabinets, led by Angela Merkel, formed by the Christian-democrats and the Social-democrats, which have had the support of more than three-fourths of voters and of members of Parliament.

The main contribution of Germany to the European Union comes from these successful democratic experiences. The best German service to Europe does not lie in attempting to become its ruler or hegemon or in making a German Europe. The best contribution of Germany is its example of decentralized, multilevel, pluralistic and consensual democracy, which has become the model for the European Union itself.

4

The Wild East

Some external borders of the European Union are porous. Oothers are not well-fixed and have become the focus of violent conflicts. In Bulgaria, what the EU's higher officer for border protection called "the most important land border of the EU" was called "Border of Death" some time ago, under the Communist regime. At that time, a wire fence sealed off Bulgaria's border to keep people in and, like in Berlin and all along Eastern Europe, to kill those who tried to escape. Twenty years or so after those barriers were removed, the Bulgarian government, drawing on money from the European Union, constructed a new border metal fence near four meters high, which will stretch 100 miles. This time the fence is to keep people out, that is, to prevent people from Africa and the Middle East from entering the EU through Turkey ad Greece.

A similar fence was previously built along the Greek border with Turkey, but the flow of hundreds of thousands of immigrants and refuge-seekers from the Middle East moved towards the Bulgarian edge. A similar fence is built at the Hungarian border with Serbia, for the same purpose. High walls also rise in Ceuta and Melilla, the Spanish enclaves in Northern Africa, to impede people from coming in from Morocco. Masses of needed people also try to cross from Africa by sea to the islands of Greece in the Aegean, Malta, Cyprus and Sicily, in many cases at the peril of death. Once on European land, they aim at moving towards France, Germany or Sweden, the dreams of their lives.

The borders of the European Union in the South are porous to immigrants because they are made of water. On the Eastern mainland, in contrast, the borders are not solid because they include frontier territories, especially with the Russian empire, which are fields for violent conflicts. Unfixed, vulnerable borders and contentious frontier lands are typical characteristics of empires. In the following pages, we will review three main land border problems of the European Union: with Turkey, as mentioned; in the Balkans, in the Southeast; and with some former Soviet republics under Russian influence.

Asiatic Turkey

Perhaps the most dramatic disappointment of the expectation to become a full member state of the European Union has happened in Turkey. This remnant of the Ottoman Empire turned strong nationalist state applied to join the European Community as long ago as in 1987 and has not achieved any clear result. In contrast, the dozen most recent members of the EU obtained accession only between five and ten years after their application.

The obstacles to Turkey's full membership derive, first of all, from its eccentric and relatively remote location in Asia Minor, except for the relatively small territory of Eastern Thrace on the European side of the Sea of Marmara. The border problems with Greece and Bulgaria above referenced would change if Turkey became a member state of the EU. But outside the physical limits of the continent the prospects for accession to the EU are grim.

It's true that the Treaty on European Union states that any country defined as European that respects the values of freedom, democracy and the rule of law may apply to become a member of the Union. Yet further expansion of the EU beyond obvious territorial confines is highly unlikely. In fact, a couple of external candidacies were rejected. Morocco's application was turned down because the European Council did "not consider Morocco a European country". Broad support for the EU among the population of Israel has been responded to with the proposal of possible integration "short of full membership."

As Turkey's foreign policy has also recently been more oriented towards becoming an influential power in the Middle East in turmoil, its European allegiance seems to have considerably vanished. But precisely as a consequence of Turkey moving away from Europe and the new arrivals of Middle Eastern and Maghrebian migrants and refugees, the Turkish border with the

EU has become a new contentious arena for fences, checkpoints and border patrols.

Turkey also has a major frontier problem with the European Union because it occupies Northern Cyprus. Since the Turkish army invaded the island in 1974, it keeps control over one-third of the territory of what is now a full member state of the Union. For several decades, the United Nations peacekeepers have maintained a "green zone" between the two parts of the country. But the division is recognized by neither state besides Turkey. Nor are the prospects for political unification of the island likely to succeed.

Location, borders, and frontiers are not the only issues about Turkey. Major obstacles for membership to the EU are also based on the country's large size, which would make it second in population in the Union. Its strongly agriculture-oriented economy might also be difficult to assimilate to certain established economic patterns. There is also the opinion that the Muslim faith of most Turkish citizens wouldn't fit certain mores of Europeans. However, this may be contradicted by the fact that there are already more than twenty million Muslims living in the

European Union, including large concentrations of them in places such as Paris and Marseille in France, Brussels, Rotterdam, as well as London and other English cities. Several other candidates to member-states of the EU in the Balkans also have Muslim majorities or very large proportions of them in the population. Rather than ethnic or religious mismatches, it is denunciations of Turkish government's violations of civil liberties that have been declared incompatible with basic criteria for EU membership.

The Caribbean in the Balkans

The Balkans Peninsula, on the Southeast of the continent, has been the scenario of violent conflicts. The region has been another major, long unsettled frontier territory of the European empire. The EU still faces the dilemma of whether not to incorporate Serbia and other countries of the former Communist Yugoslavia that were at war in the 1990s.

Yugoslavia was created as a multi-ethnic federation, initially dominated by the Serbs. Under

Communist rule, and in order to disperse the Serbs and prevent the largest group from smashing the minorities, the Yugoslav federation was restructured into a conglomerate of four languages, five nations, six republics, and eight political units with equal powers in central government. But after the fall of Communism in the late 1980s, the project of "Serbian reunification" reemerged, and ethnic conflict arose.

Yugoslavia collapsed in a very disorderly manner. Slovenia, a former member of the Austrian empire in the Northwest of the country, declared independence in 1991 and was the first to join the EU and NATO. The independence of Croatia one year later provoked a long and very bloody clash between Serbs and Croats in the war of Bosnia-Herzegovina. "Ethnic cleansing" also took place in Kosovo in 1999. Hundreds of thousands of ethnic Albanians fled from Kosovo and took refuge in Macedonia, where insurgency and violence also exploded in 2001. United Nations' and European Union intervention and NATO's bombings eventually pacified the area. Under international supervision, Montenegro was legally permitted to vote for its independence in 2006.

The disordered dissolution of Yugoslavia was not followed by an orderly process of integration of the Balkan Peninsula in Europe. Currently, Slovenia and Croatia are full member-states of the European EU. Official candidates and officially potential candidates include all the remaining former members of the federation: Serbia, Bosnia and Herzegovina, Macedonia, Montenegro, Kosovo, as well as enclosed Albania. All these countries belong to the Stabilization and Association Agreement, which gives them access to the EU's markets and financial support. They should be able to adapt to EU rules and processes at not insurmountable costs, as the region is now completely circled by EU territory and the total population of its six countries amounts to only about five percent of the total population of the EU. Yet, the hypothetical future membership of some candidates is made to be contingent on pending democratization and institutionalization.

The European Commission has recently established that no new member state will be accepted at least before 2020. This may create better opportunities for the Union to advance and consolidate higher internal cohesion on new policy fields. Yet a failure to integrate most of the Balkans may also imply the persistence of conflicts and violence. As it is, the region risks becoming the Caribbean of Europe, that is, a set of geographically close but never fully integrated countries with long-lasting internal instability, mass emigration, and recurrent hostility to the EU. The European Union is not interested in having a Cuba or a Haiti near its borders. But the incompleteness of the territory on that side of the continent is likely to last.

The Russian Frontier

Just after his inauguration in December 2014, the President of the European Council, Donald Tusk, declared "Russia is our strategic problem". The eastern frontier of the EU is the greatest example of the problems that two rival empires have to face to establish fixed borders between them. As after the Cold War the borders of the European Union moved eastwards, the spheres of influence of the

West and Russia needed to be redefined. But, on one side, the Russian empire shrank, and it's in a process of trying to reverse the humiliation. On the other side, the European empire has not discarded plans for further expansion.

Both the European Union and the Russian Federation hold mutually incompatible plans for potential additions of military allies and economic partners. One could say that none of the two empires is currently "imperialistic" in the traditional sense of the word, that is, they don't aim at conquering and maintaining direct control over territories by force. But some asymmetry exists. Recovering from imperial shrinkage is more important for Russia than any further expansion is for the EU. This means that the authoritarian Russian empire cares more about the limits of its rival's influence, which, after the painful defeat in the Cold War, is still seen as a permanent threat. But the European empire is likely not to be willing to engage in direct military conflicts near its already extended borders.

A temporary agreement between the two blocs was reached between the US President, Bill Clinton, and the elected leader of the new Russian

Federation, Boris Yeltsin, in the mid-1990s. In Clinton's words:

> "I told Yeltsin that if he would agree to NATO-expansion [with Czech Republic, Hungary, Poland and other former members of the Soviet-dominated Warsaw Pact] and the NATO-Russia partnership, I would make a commitment not to station troops or missiles in the new countries prematurely, and to support Russia membership in the new Group of Eight (G-8), the World Trade Organization, and other international organizations. We had a deal."

Accordingly, Russia was formally accepted as a member of the G-7, which began to be called G-8, in 1997. In the following years, the EU and NATO developed concrete plans for further enlargements with former Communist East European countries. The initial deal implied that there would be an intermediate buffer zone between EU and NATO member states and Russia's sphere of influence, formed by most Western former members of the Soviet Union (with the exception of the three Baltic republics).

The deal was implicitly renewed at the first encounter between the new US President George W. Bush and the new Russian President Vladimir Putin, in 2001. Putin was reluctant to accept NATO's new missile plans (after the "premature" period forecasted by Clinton). But both presidents said that they had found the basis for a relationship of "mutual respect and cooperation".

As planned, NATO gradually accepted as new members 12 former allies of the Warsaw Pact and developed new partnerships with Russia and all the former Soviet republics. But by the end of US President Bush's second mandate, in 2008, NATO also considered admitting former Soviet republics Georgia and Ukraine as allies. One year later, the European Union launched an Eastern Partnership program offering six former republics of the Soviet Union —Armenia, Azerbaijan, Belarus, Georgia, Moldova and Ukraine— free trade agreements and "full integration short of membership" in exchange for internal economic and political reforms.

These offers clashed with the plans of the new rulers in Moscow to rebuild the Russian empire. Vladimir Putin had declared the dissolution of the

Soviet Union "the greatest geopolitical catastrophe of the twentieth century", and he was determined to recover from it. During the breakup of the Soviet Union, at the initiative of Russia, most former Soviet republics had formed a Commonwealth of Independent States (CIS). A subset of them also formed a military alliance called Collective Security Treaty Organization, from which Georgia eventually withdrew. Russia also promoted the formation of a CIS Free Trade Area in 2011. After the withdrawal of Ukraine and Moldova, it became the Eurasian Economic Union in 2014, basically formed around Russia by Belarus, Kazakhstan, Kyrgyzstan, as well as Armenia when it quit the Eastern Partnership of the EU.

All these countries' entrances and withdrawals to and from Western and Eastern alliances and unions have, of course, occurred through eventful changes in domestic politics of the countries involved. They have included electoral overthrowing of governments, poisoning of foreign politicians, ousting of elected presidents, "orange" and "rose" revolutions, jailing of opposition leaders, hasty referendums, armed rebellions, military invasions, and martial coups.

Belarus –previously called Byelo-Russia— has been a less contentious territory because it has been long ruled by a dictator who seriously considers the union with Russia under a single common government. But when Georgia hinted with shifting sides and becoming a member of NATO in 2008, the Russian army immediately occupied the secessionist Georgian regions of Abkhazia and South Ossetia and recognized them as independent countries. Likewise, after Ukraine left the CIS Free Trade Area and reached a free trade and political association agreement with the European Union in 2013, the Russian army occupied the former Russian and at the time Ukrainian Peninsula of Crimea, which declared its independence and joined the Russian Federation the following year. As a new Ukrainian president signed the agreement with the EU, Russia supported armed rebellions against the Ukrainian government within the transfrontier Euroregion Donbass, which includes the Russian area of Rostov, as well as the Ukrainian lands of Donetsk and Lugansk where independent republics were proclaimed.

In fact, Russia has some direct borders with EU territories without intermediate cushions: with Finland, Estonia and Latvia, and also with Lithuania and Poland in the Russian enclave of Kaliningrad. Further plans might include Russia's cooption of Ukrainian territories up to connect with Transnistria, the secessionist territory of Moldova supported by the Russian government, which could lead Russia to border on EU territory in Romania too. Following the precedent set by Crimea, the Transnistrian parliament asked to join the Russian Federation.

The temporary post-Cold War compromise was more formally terminated in 2014 with the expulsion of Russia from the G-8, which became the G-7 again. On the Western side, the plans for further enlargements of NATO with former Soviet republics were, de facto, abandoned. The EU's partnership and cooperation agreement with Belarus was not concluded, and bilateral relations and technical assistance programs were frozen. The enforcement of the trade and association agreement of the EU with Ukraine was suspended.

The association and trade agreement with Moldova is pending of ratification.

Yet, further maneuvers show that the redefinition of the frontier between the European Union and former lands of the Soviet Union is still pending. Western economic sanctions against Russia, NATO's military exercises in the Black Sea, together with barely veiled military interventions of Russia in several former Soviet republics, keep making the EU's unsettled frontier the Wild East of the Union. Like the American frontier in the legendary Wild West of the mid-nineteenth century, the area is likely to be characterized for a long while by weak institutions, propensity to civil unrest, disorder, crime, banditry, extrajudicial retribution and lawless violence.

Shaking Imperial Frontiers

An inter-imperial frontier typically thwarts the sovereignty of the territories affected. A relatively stable settlement can be reached by two rival empires by their mutual acceptance of the neutrality of some intermediately located countries.

This was, for example, the case of Austria or Finland during the Cold War, which, while being democratic and prosperous countries, remained outside both NATO and the Warsaw Pact. As after the Cold War the borders of the European empire moved eastwards to absorb former Communist countries, the intermediate frontier with the Russian empire could also be moved in the same direction and leave Belarus, Ukraine and Moldova non-aligned, as was implicitly assumed in the Clinton-Yeltsin agreement in the 1990s.

Yet it should be recalled that the frontier of the Cold War was also set within German lands and at the Berlin's Wall, which was a focus of hostility and tensions for several decades. Analogously, new "walls" are also raised nowadays within the countries that could become intermediate buffers between Europe and Russia, as the two empires have not discarded further expansions and the populations hold opposite allegiances, which keep them living in turmoil.

Establishing clear limits of the European Union would certainly favor stability and peace. An EU's foreign policy with significant influence in the world would be feasible to develop only if it went beyond the problems of defining its own borders. However, unsettled frontiers, which are typical of empires, are likely to persist so that those are not results that may be reached soon.

5

What Has Europe Done for Us?

The European Empire is frequently criticized for lackluster delivery. It has been blamed for lack of competitiveness, economic stagnation, mass unemployment, weak foreign policy, among other failures. Sometimes, these criticisms evoke a discussion about the accomplishments of another major empire, Rome, as was portrayed in Monty Python's satirical film *Life of Brian*.

Let me transcribe a fanciful, celebrated scene. The leader of one of the fractions of the Jewish resistance agsnst the Empire, Reg, is addressing potential followers. He rhetorically asks: "What, after all, have the Romans ever done for us?"

Then the people in the audience interrupt the speaker and respond by outlining all forms of positive aspects of the occupation by the Roman Empire:

"-- The aqueduct?

Reg: What?

-- The aqueduct.

Reg: Oh. Yeah, yeah. They did give us that. Uh, that's true. Yeah."

But the followers follow up: And the sanitation. And the roads. Irrigation. Medicine. Education. Public baths. And the wine...

"And it's safe to walk in the streets at night now, Reg" --ads another.

"Yeah, they certainly know how to keep order. Let's face it. They're the only ones who could in a place like this."

"Heh heh heh", giggle the followers.

So that Reg summarizes:

"All right, but apart from the sanitation, the medicine, education, wine, public order, irrigation, roads, a fresh water system, and public health... what have the Romans ever done for us?

-- Brought peace.

Reg: Oh. Peace? Shut up!'"

Nowadays in the European Empire it seems as if some people could also ask: What, after all, has Europe ever done for us? The list of achievements would be as impressive as the one of the Roman Empire was for the Jews. Let's sketch a few. The European Union has indeed delivered the following:

A broad open market to producers and consumers. Freedom of movement of goods, services, capitals and workers, including the possibility to choose where to live and to have professional qualifications recognized.

A common currency and monetary policy. Control of certain monopolistic practices. A policy of balanced budgets to prevent waste of public resources. And oversight, supervision and sustainability of private banks.

Beyond these measures oriented to liberalizing markets, the EU has also delivered legislation on female equal pay and four-week holiday entitlement, vast agriculture subsidies, investments in infrastructures, and funds to underdeveloped countries and regions. Not a mean achievement, indeed.

But the EU has also brought non-economic goods, including freedom of travel without border control. It has made air travel cheaper and tourism easier and has reduced the price of making phone calls abroad. It has also made beaches cleaner. And it has opened forever the minds, horizons and opportunities of one and a half million young people who have completed part of their studies in another member state thanks to the Erasmus program.

Actually, the EU has favored and promoted nothing less than democratization and compliance with the rule of law in about half of its current member-states, which were controlled by dictatorial regimes not so long ago. The death penalty has been abolished in all cases and under all circumstances.

And the Union has brought peace. Oh yes, peace, don't forget that, please. Because, after all, peace, instead of a succession of increasingly frequent and lethal intra-European wars, has been the most important change in the life of Europeans in several centuries.

Step by step

The European Union did not deliver all those public goods with a single stroke. They are rather the result of a long process that was not entirely planned or anticipated from the beginning. Some strategies for increasing integration have not been as fortunate as others. To clarify the current state of the Union and to try a forecast, it is worth to review how some strategies have succeeded, and others have failed so far. Three basic approaches to fostering European integration that have been tried can be called: federalism, step-by-step, and stop-and-go.

The first, federalism, had its moment after the shock of World War II. As mentioned in a previous chapter, some idealist activists advocated the rapid construction of a European federal state. The European Federalist Movement crafted its foundational manifesto, mainly by anti-fascist resistant Altiero Spinelli, still during the war. It intended to oppose "the restoration of the national state" and to build, in contrast, a European federation conceived as "a solid international State" in control of European armed forces, security and economy. In other words, the aim was the "definitive abolition of division of Europe into national, sovereign states". Spinelli would become a member of the European Parliament and of the European Commission in the 1970s when the federalist movement pressured with some success for specific reforms, including the direct election of the Parliament. But it's fairly apparent that the maximalist objectives of the European federalists – the abolition of national states-- have not dominated the agenda of most significant decision-makers in the EU.

More sensible was the further plan to advance "step-by-step". According to it, the European integration would start with a few crucial issues in the hands of states. It was expected then that subsequent technical requirements and newly created solidarity would augment the willingness to proceed with continually increasing integration on other issues. This alternative approach was already conceived a few years after the end of World War II. Federalist Jean Monnet acknowledged that, in contrast to prior expectations, "Europe will not be made all at once, or accounting to a single plan". Then he began to envisage a long march, step by step.

The first attempt was with the paramount issue of security, that is, military integration of the foremost European states to prevent a major new war. Monnet persuaded the French foreign affairs minister, Robert Schuman, to start uniting the coal and steel industries of France and Germany –the traditional enemies at war—under a single authority. This would make war "materially impossible". The corresponding specialized Coal and Steel Community was created in 1952, on the assumption that it would be "a first step in the federation of Europe", in Monnet's words. Later on, an Atomic Energy Community (Euratom) would also be created with the aim of limiting the use of atomic energy only for peaceful purposes. In parallel, the French government promoted the creation of a European Defense Community with its own European army. But the plan failed to obtain ratification by the French National Assembly in 1954.

The following year, Germany, the main loser of World War II, was accepted as a member of the winning military alliance, the North Atlantic Treaty Organization. This decision put the whole West European defense and security affairs in the hands of the transatlantic organization. The security issue proved to be not strictly European, but global. Against Monnet and others' hopes, the attempt at building a Europe-wide security system didn't become a first step in a process of further European integration. Nevertheless, the weakness of Europe in the ability to guarantee its security and defense would be resented for many years.

Much more successful to foster the union of Europe was the issue of trade. New technologies for transport and communication created new opportunities for commerce at large scale and generated increasing economic interdependence among major industrial countries. In Europe, the degree of interdependence was particularly intense, in correspondence to its high levels of economic activity, reconstruction and growth.

The institutional response was the creation of the European Economic Community, usually known as "the Common Market", in 1957. In its founding Treaty of Rome it was conceived "to lay the foundation of an ever closer union". Monnet expected now that it would be the common market that would become "the beginning of the road", that is a start able to launch "a chain reaction, a ferment where one change includes another".

The same technological and structural incentives that had favored the expansion of trade incentivized capital movements for investments and financial transactions across state borders. In a further step in the integration process, the subsequent institutional adaption would be the abolition of exchange controls. Further on, the abolition of internal borders provoked demands for an area of security and justice, which was shaped by the Schengen agreement.

Other steps followed, in particular regarding currencies. The international system of monetary stability adopted in Bretton Woods at the end of World War II had been abandoned in the early 1970s. Each national currency engaged in competitive devaluations against the others, which distorted international trade, as well as common European policies implying monetary transfers, such as agriculture subsidies.

The reactions to the monetary crisis passed through a series of stages. First, all major European countries restricted the relative fluctuations of their currencies within a "currency snake". Then, they pegged their currencies to each other with fixed exchange rates in the so-called European Monetary Union from 1979 on. And they created the euro, which became the only legal common currency in 1999 while actual euro notes and coins have been issued since 2002. Most countries adopted the common currency and shaped the Euro-zone, but other member states of the Union remained outside.

Stop-and-go

There have been, thus, moves forward. But the union of Europe has not advanced all together and at sustained speed, as had been planned and expected by Monnet and the technocratic federalists, also called "functionalists." The EU's journey has not been like following directions step by step, but rather like driving at rush hour with heavy traffic: quite unhurriedly and at irregular paces. Even if some drivers are located in the fast lane, they can only temporarily move and often have to drive slowly. Rather than linear progress in increasing integration, there have been varying speeds on different issues and several stops-and-goes.

A crucial challenge was the economic and financial crisis that exploded in 2008 and the subsequent Great Recession. Gigantic financial bubbles had been fostered in the United States and Europe following high liberalization of trade, capital mobility and bank investments, together with low-interest rates. Firms, families and banks contracted huge amounts of private debt. In Europe, the first big bubbles, mostly formed of housing mortgages and other bank loans, began to burst in Ireland, Greece, and Spain.

Then, hundreds of banks all across Europe were rescued with state governments' funds. Depending on the country, about one third or one fourth of private debt was transformed into public debt by governments willing to save business in peril. In turn, some private banks bought new public debt. All across Europe, both private and public finances turned out to be gigantic, highly interdependent and enormously dislocated.

The European Union had established caps on the Euro-zone states' public deficit and public debt (3% and 60% of GDP, respectively) in the so-called Stability and Growth Pact in the 1990s. In fact, several countries, including France and Germany, had run public deficits beyond the committed limits. While the economy was buoyant, and extra debts seemed easily payable, the European Commission looked away. But when the new public deficits became unbearable and debts and loans engendered by governments' responses to the crisis had to be reimbursed, the EU began to pool states' fiscal policy.

Most countries were able to contain or reduce their public deficits within the agreed limit, including balanced or near balanced budgets in Germany, Austria, Denmark, Estonia, Lithuania and Luxembourg. In contrast, the public finances of Cyprus, Greece, Ireland and Portugal, as well as some over-indebted private banks of Spain, had to be rescued under command by the European Commission and the European Central Bank with rather reluctant additional aid from the International Monetary Fund –a set of institutions nicknamed "the troika".

As a consequence of these operations, increasing EU powers were consolidated. Loans and bailouts to state members were approved by the "troika" conditional to the introduction by state governments of structural reforms. With the intention of improving the productivity of the country's economy and the subsequent state's capacity to bear financial obligations, the induced reforms affect state-owned enterprises, social spending, labor markets, red tape for business and other issues. A new Fiscal Stability Treaty, also known as the Fiscal Compact, which is enforced since 2013, made the balanced budget a general norm. It also established that the Euro-zone states' annual draft budgets must be approved by the European Commission before being submitted to national parliaments.

Regarding private finances, a European banking union was also eventually agreed upon. The role of banks in the European economy is stronger than in the United States or other developed countries. They gather together about 300% of the Euro-zone GDP and provide about 70% of firms' external financing. By a new unified system established in 2014, the European Central Bank became the only oversight and supervisor of the 130 largest private banks all across Europe (which account for about 80% of all assets in the European banking system). This should ensure that, in the future, at least the major banks will hold enough capital to prevent new bankruptcies. In case of a bank crisis requiring its rescue, restructuring or shut down, an independent Single Resolution Mechanism will make the decision on how to share losses. With this, the only remaining traditional powers of national central banks in the Euro-zone were pooled. The Mechanism was also adapted to the division between countries inside and outside the Euro-zone by requiring a majority support in each group to make enforceable decisions.

In the long term, there has been, thus, a cumulative process from the common market to open borders, monetary, fiscal and banking unions. But every step has required increasing negotiation costs and has produced greater asymmetric results, as not all countries have been willing to follow all the successive steps. All in all, it is true that, more or less like in initial federal dreams, a gradual integration has been built over time in Europe. But the process has been much slower than the federalists desired in the aftermath of the World War; it has stalled around some particularly contentious issues; it has left behind numerous countries all along the way; and it's far from being completed even for those that move ahead.

6

Multiple Speeds

In the peculiar jargon of Brussels bureaucrats and EU pundits, there is a lot of talk of union by means of "variable geometry", "concentric circles", "multi-speed", "flexible' or "a la carte". It is also imagined that, in consequence, they may produce "a strong core", "a junction box", "a house in the garden" or a "poliphony". These and other fancy or odd metaphors refer to different degrees of integration of different countries on different times and on different issues, as mentioned in the previous chapter, which can be explained by the different degrees of harmony or conflict of interests.

In order to understand the problem of asymmetric integration, let's examine the priorities recently selected by the European Commission for the next few years. First, one of the Commission's objectives, the building of a digital single market for citizens and business, should be within reach. It shouldn't be more difficult than building the single market for goods and capitals, as everybody can obtain benefit from easier and better communications. It requires to knock down barriers on telecommunication regulations, copyrights, data protection standards, management of radio waves, and so on. The aim is the elimination of previously existing regulations at the state level, rather than the introduction of new ones.

In contrast, the energy union –which is postulated by the Commission at the same level of importance-- is likely to be much more contentious. It's clear that some states have very different interests on the issue. The United Kingdom is the largest producer of oil; France is heavily reliant on nuclear generation; Germany and Spain have favored renewable; Poland focuses on coal; and Eastern countries are highly dependent on crude oil and natural gas from Russia. There are few electrical and gas interconnectors across countries in Europe. Higher integration to favor transfers of energy and the adoption of common rules for taxes and tariffs would increase efficiency and greatly reduce consumer prices. Yet the stakes are high and multi-state negotiations are slow and no primrose path.

Other issues also raise high levels of conflict of interests between countries and can make further integration more difficult than some of those achieved in the past.

Following the logic of an ever closer union, further steps could include, for instance, the labor market and social security systems (as they are integrated, in particular, in the United States). Different regulations are, indeed, enforced in different countries regarding issues such as minimum wage, types of work contracts, collective bargaining, the role of workers' unions, retirement age, etc. Although in most states vast portions of public spending are concentrated on pensions, unemployment benefits, medical care and other social subsidies, high variation of volumes, coverage and formulas across countries exists. Partly as a consequence of disparate regulations and formulas, huge country differences can be observed in unemployment rates.

However, common legislation on labor market and social security is not even under consideration in the European Union, as it would not only be financially costly, but would also imply major social redistributions. Every state has a kind of veto power on any EU draft legislative act that could affect "the scope, cost or financial structure" of its national social security system.

These and other issues are less integrated than the markets, the currency and the fiscal and financial policies not because the European scale for their provision would be less efficient. The reason is that, in contrast to previous integrative steps, they would require major redistributions and transfers of fiscal resources from the states to the Union, which imply high levels of conflicts of interests among countries.

Asymmetric commitments

Every decision to increase European integration on a new issue has responded to new challenges and opportunities for which the previously existing institutions were not prepared. As is usually noted, the union of Europe has always advanced by responses to crises. But technical demands and global efficiency criteria are not sufficient mechanisms to induce states to cede powers to the Union. Each major crisis has required specific bargains among state governments to accept pooling their decision powers and the design of new rules and institutions. The result is not a compact, homogeneous federation, but notorious asymmetries among countries regarding their commitments to common policies on certain issues.

At the beginning of the European Economic Community, the Council of Ministers formed by state representatives made decisions by unanimity, which implied respect of each state's sovereignty. This procedure was operational regarding some relatively harmonious issues, such as trade liberalization, in which everybody could expect to obtain some positive gains. But as new issues involve more diverse interests and require redistributive decisions, the unanimity rule was gradually replaced with less demanding requirements through a series of new treaties.

As alternatives to unanimous agreements, the EU has used the allocation of weighted votes to the countries on the basis of their population size, as well as qualified majority decision rules requiring super-majority supports of winning proposals. On most issues, decisions have to be made in agreement by the Council representing the states and the directly elected European Parliament. The EU also uses open methods of coordination in policy areas with high differences among countries that are called rather odd names such as framework directives, soft law, co-regulation, or voluntary agreements.

In fact, different countries have obtained different relative returns on different issues, greatly depending on their specializations. The countries with more intense interests on some issues usually receive the largest concessions from other negotiators, while they may concede more on other issues. For example, France and Italy particularly benefitted from agriculture policy. The United Kingdom, Spain, and the post-Communist countries, from regional and structural funds subsidizing disadvantaged sectors. Germany, from the euro and the banking union. And so on. The result of countries' different interests and advantages on different issues and less-than-unanimous decisions is that countries have been integrated to different degrees.

The asymmetries of commitments on different issues do explicitly permit the exclusion of some countries from certain agreements. Officially, the EU allows "enhanced cooperation" among subsets of member-states if at least nine of them share an intense interest on some issue even if no other states are involved. While some major issues have not integrated certain countries, some non-members of the EU share certain common policies with the more integrated states. In other words: some member states f the EU 'opt out' some common policies, while some non-member states 'opt in' some of those policies.

Temporary absences have existed regarding social policies and human rights. But currently, major differences regard defense and security, the common currency, and border control. Specifically, the military alliance formed since the late 1940s under the umbrella of the United States,

NATO, does not include seven EU member states, some of which were formally neutral during the Cold War. They are Austria, Croatia, Cyprus, Finland, Ireland, Malta and Sweden. At the same time, NATO includes a few non-EU members: Norway and Turkey, as well as, of course, the transatlantic United States and Canada.

Likewise, the common currency, the euro, and the common monetary policy of the European Central Bank do not include nine EU member-states. Outside, the United Kingdom, which left the European Exchange Rate Mechanism after the sterling pound came under major pressures by currency speculators in the early 1990s, never joined the euro. Denmark also negotiated a formal 'opt-out' much in advance, although its currency, the krone, continues to be pegged to the euro.

All other members of the EU are required by treaty eventually to join the euro, but seven countries do not seem to be on that path. Some people have raised the suspicion that some, like Sweden, for instance, intentionally violate some technical criteria that are required to join, such as central bank independence. But probably such ruses are not needed, as it's not an EU priority to pressure any new country to join soon. In contrast, half a dozen non-member micro-states use the euro as their only currency (Andorra, Kosovo, Monaco, Montenegro, San Marino, and the Vatican).

Similarly, the Schengen agreements on border control, police and judicial cooperation, which were incorporated into EU law in 1997, are not shared by six member-states, but adopted by a few non-EU members. Out are the United Kingdom and Ireland, which keep their common border open through Northern Ireland. Also four recent members: Bulgaria, Croatia, Cyprus, and Romania, which are excluded by the Union for failing to implement previous commitments regarding their judicial and corruption systems. In contrast, the border control agreement is signed by Iceland, Norway, Switzerland, and applied by most micro-states.

All in all, there are EU members that are not NATO members, others are in the euro but not in Schengen, others not in the euro but in Schengen, others neither in euro nor in Schengen, and non-EU members that are in either NATO or in euro or in Schengen or in several of these unions.

Rather than uniform European integration, there are nowadays different degrees of union across issues and countries. This type of asymmetry is likely to endure. In the future, different countries may keep accepting further integration on new issues along different paths and at different speeds. They may keep driving by stops-and-goes. The way forward may involve the formation of "coalitions of the willing", that is, groups of countries prepared to pool more powers and resources in specific areas, which may, nevertheless, be open to late joiners. These unbalances are, indeed, typical of empires.

7

Too Much Regulation, Too Little Budget

As we have seen in the last two chapters, the European Union has done very much for us, perhaps too much, according to some people. For some other people, however, it still does too little and much more should be done.

On the one hand, the European Union is frequently accused of enacting excessive bans, restrictions, and regulations. Some British tabloids, in particular, do not miss an occasion to denounce unacceptable intrusions of "the bureaucrats in Brussels" into the private lives of European citizens. Scandalous instances have included, for example, the standardization of the flushing of toilets and urinals, the diktat ordering bar-maids' cleavages to be covered, or the rules about the length, shape and curvature of bananas and cucumbers. Actually, these famous 'regulations' never existed or were eventually dropped.

But more seriously, the amount of legislative production of the European Union is considerable. It can be estimated that, in most countries, about half of national legislation with significant economic impact enacted every year, counting both parliamentary laws and administrative acts by the executive, is derived from the EU. (See 'Sources' for details).

On the other hand, the EU's performance has been disappointing on several respects. They include, for example, the 'Lisbon Agenda', which was adopted in 2000 with the intention to make the EU in ten years "the most competitive and dynamic knowledge-based economy in the world". The EU is also recurrently accused of not having done much for the victims of the more recent economic Great Recession, such as the enormous numbers of unemployed youth in certain countries, or for the mass waves of people escaping from war in the Middle East and crossing borders in search of refuge.

In fact, the European Union cannot do very much because its resources are paltry. The EU's annual budget amounts to about 1% of the Gross European Product, while the average member state (including regional and local governments) spends about 48% of its Gross Domestic Product.

Actually, the two blames for too much and too little intervention are two sides of the same coin. Europe is overregulated precisely because the Union suffers from insufficient resources of its own. Note that, in fact, the most important steps in European integration previously reviewed dealt with low-cost or even saving issues. The dramatic reduction in the size of state armies and military spending after the Cold War was not accompanied by the building of a new costly European army. The abolition of barriers to capital movements or the suppression of border controls permitted significant savings in administrative costs. Replacing national currencies with the euro didn't require setting a costly administrative apparatus. And so this has been the case regarding other issues, such as harmonization of standards or regulation of competitive markets.

Above all, the EU's overregulation of the states' fiscal policy –including their annual budget previsions of revenues and expenditures-- is strongly related to Brussels' scanty availability of financial resources. In the absence of a solid Europe-wide fiscal system, the EU substitutes regulations for funds. More precisely put, it substitutes overregulation of states' fiscal policy for its own fiscal resources. That's why too little EU resources force too much regulation.

The learning experience of the United States

The current fiscal relations between the European Union and the member-states are the opposite of those in the United States. In the US, the federal government is financially stronger than the states, in contrast to the weakness of the EU regarding its member states. At the same time, and in spite of some appearances, Washington regulates much less over the states than Brussels does over the member-states of the EU. As the US federal government in Washington is much more resourceful than the EU institutions in Brussels are, it can develop its own large-scale policies and it does not need to intrude in the policy-making of the states.

As a result of low federal intrusion and states' autonomy, there is a remarkable legislative disparity among the states of the US on some issues. Legislative variety among states is particularly notable on contract, property, family, and criminal law, including, for example, taxes, abortion, gun ownership or the death penalty. The key is that Washington is more powerful than Brussels and, thanks to that, it does not need to oversee, supervise and protect the states as much as Brussels does in Europe. As a consequence, the states in the US are also more responsible for some of their own decisions --especially regarding their financial viability-- than are the member-states of the EU.

This has not always been like this. Building the American union required a very long process of gradual, conflict-ridden and asymmetric integration that may evoke the ongoing process in the EU. At the beginning of its existence by the late eighteenth century, the United States federal government was extremely weak, as weak as the European Union can be now in terms of fiscal resources. The bulk of spending, including for the wars for independence against the British, relied upon the states, which had proclaimed their sovereignty before agreeing to form the Union.

After the wars, the US Treasury, initially led by Alexander Hamilton, decided to mutualize the huge debts of the states –that is, to create federal debt able to absorb the state debts. The federal government began, thus, to increase its strength at the expense of the states by exchanging debt payments for power. Later on, the institutions in Washington also made important direct investments in infrastructures along the westward expansion of the country. The maximum interference of the federal government in some states' domestic policies took place, of course, around the Civil War, which led to suppressing slavery in the Southern states. Later on, a permanent federal income tax was created.

But the federal government achieved control of more than half of total public expenditure for the first time as late as in 1940 –that is, about 150 years after its creation-- as a consequence of the expansion of the public sector against the Great Depression. Only since then has the US government had sufficient fiscal resources to develop broad federal programs in defense, infrastructures, social security, health care, and research and development. In contrast to the EU, the US federal government has also been able to quickly put broad stimulus against recessions into effect, most recently since 2009.

In the US, the relatively high federal spending has redistributive effects, especially because social security favors people in less advanced states. An index to measure redistribution of financial resources by public powers is the fiscal balances of the states with the Federation. That is the difference between what the citizens of each state pay in federal taxes and what they receive from federal expenses. The fiscal balances are very different for different states, negative for some, like Minnesotta or New York, for example, and positive for others, like Missouri or New Mexico, for other examples, with imbalances reaching up to two figure percentage points. In some states the balance has changed sign over time, in some cases both ways –including, for instance, Texas, which is strongly dependent on oil international prices--, depending on the ups and downs of the state's economy. Largely as a consequence of federal policies, the inequality in citizens' disposable per capita income across states is nowadays much lower than it was about one hundred years ago. The maximum difference in per capita income among citizens of different US states is in a proportion of about 2:1.

The other side of the story is that, along this process of strengthening the resources of the federal government, the US stopped giving financial aid to states or cities in bankruptcy since 1840. Thousands of local governments have defaulted, especially after the Civil War, during the Great Depression, and most recently in California, Illinois or Detroit, for example. The local government debt is never mutualized, and states and cities are allowed to default by themselves without federal rescues or bailouts.

In this context of federal irresponsibility for the condition of states' finances, almost all member states have adopted criteria of financial responsibility. In particular, they have adopted balanced budgets amendments to their constitutions. The states became financially self-sufficient during the nineteenth century after their war debts were rescued. The states regained power in exchange for fiscal responsibility, which implied the obligation to assume their further own debts. Nowadays they are pretty free to develop their own public policies on a number of issues.

European Greece vs American Puerto Rico

In order to understand how consequential are the differences between the European Union and the United States just presented, let's compare the recent turnabouts of Greece and Puerto Rico, two countries of relatively small or medium-size with similar huge economic and public debt problems. They represent two major alternatives to deal with the crisis: default and bailout.

Puerto Rico has been for default. In 2015 the Governor and most people of the island wanted to declare bankruptcy. But as Puerto Rico is not a state but only a "Commonwealth" of the US, they were seeking support from candidates to the next US presidential election to legalize that option. The governor and the legislators of Puerto Rico dealt with the crisis by designing and implementing by themselves, without federal intervention, harsh measures oriented to increase public revenues and reduce spending. The other alternative, bailout by the federal government, was out of question, as has been in almost every case in the US for a very long while, as explained above.

Greece, in contrast, was for successive bailouts from the EU both when the government was led by center-right, by center-left and the by far left parties. Even when a referendum on the EU's bailout in 2015 produced a majority of voters against, the government accepted the bailout and the annexed Memorandum of Understanding with the European Commission. Virtually all Greek policies on taxes, pensions, health care, control of the banks, labor market, competition, energy, administration, justice against corruption and several others were designed and committed to be implemented "over many years". In fact, Greece became a protectorate of the European Union. Its sovereignty was replaced by the EU's "suzerainty"

–as it was termed in the Ottoman Empire--. Greece's further elections and institutions have been reduced to choose the domestic rulers that will implement the decisions of the European Empire.

Neither Puerto Rico nor Greece seriously considered a third option: exit from the larger union, respectively the US and the EU. In Puerto Rico the most recent plebiscite and referendum on its status as a country was in 2012. It included 2 questions with 2+4 answers and the result was a kind of draw between keeping the current status and statehood in the US, while independence got less than 4% of votes. Greece, in turn, avoided exit from the euro and the EU by accepting the EU's bailout. As the minister of finances of the time, Yanis Varoufakis, confessed, the Greek government would be incompetent if it were left on its own. "If we manage to handle properly a Grexit—he said-- it would be possible to have an alternative. But I'm not sure we would manage it, because managing the collapse of a monetary union takes a great deal of expertise, and I'm not sure we have it here in Greece without the help of outsiders."

This may not be highly surprising, as it tells of the relative strength of the European Union and the unfitness of Greek outdated state apparatuses with an interdependent Europe. But what is more puzzling is why the EU didn't consider and the Greek governments eluded a possible default or declaration of bankruptcy of Greece within the EU and the euro. If Greece would have done like Puerto Rico –declaring bankruptcy while remaining within the larger union and the common currency areas-- its rulers would have been challenged to undertake their own way to recovery. The subsequent reforms would probably have been as harsh as those imposed by the Memorandum of Understanding. But instead of becoming an EU's protectorate, some basic tenets of democracy would have been remained alive in the country that invented such form of government.

Default within the Union may still be an option for future crises. The EU needs to confirm that it has learned from the ways the Great Recession was addressed and it will not implement large bailouts on countries in crisis next time, be either Greece again or any other country. This would mean that the institutions in Brussels would have become more self-confident and also that the states would be more respected regarding their real concerns and competences.

8

A Faustian Bargain

The current level of resources of the European Union resembles that of the United States in the late eighteenth century and early nineteenth century –the period of "empire", previous to the actual federation. The EU's fiscal resources are so meager that it cannot effectively develop by itself counter-cyclical economic policies, including vast direct spending to stimulate the economy and prevent or reverse a recession by boosting employment. It's the states that control the bulk of taxes and expenditures, like the states in the US did about two hundred years ago.

But some European states –like the US states by that time-- have contracted huge debts that they can barely repay. The EU's member states in debt wish to be rescued at the expense of all the others —as actually happened in the US. Some European states have been more prone to embark on irresponsible financial adventures because some of their rulers thought that if they eventually risked default they could always blame the Union and ask for its rescue with pooled funds from the other states. But in contrast to the situation in the US at that time, the EU has not created its own debt able to mutualize the public debts of the states (although, also in contrast to the US at the time, the EU already has a central bank that could facilitate such a major innovation).

That's why the EU had to impose oversight, regulation and control of states' finances, including a mandate for balanced budgets. Since 2010, the Euro-zone states received pointed suggestions to adopt a balanced budget mandate into its national legislation, preferably at the constitutional level. Since 2013 the European Commission controls the state budgets. It initially focused on the magnitudes of projected deficits and debts, but it has gradually paid attention to specific expenditures, taxes and other revenues, which has been a highly controversial move. In some countries, EU directives determine most of the parliament's agenda regarding the annual budget and many economic and social policies. Domestic institutions rubber-stamp a higher number of relevant fiscal choices made by the EU institutions than before the crisis.

The compulsory adoption of responsible fiscal behavior in the EU may be less effective than in the US because most member-states of the American union gradually committed to self-discipline on their own initiative. After having experienced the drama of their own bankruptcy or default, they learned the lesson and internalized the norm as part of their political culture.

Actually some European states may have already entered a debt bubble from which nobody may be able to rescue them next time. Perhaps some EU member states would need a default to be able to regain their fiscal autonomy and responsibility, as many states and cities did in the US. A foremost candidate may be Italy, which is the second country in public debt as percentage of its GDP, after Greece, and, as the country's size and economy are much bigger, its absolute debt is near seven times higher than Greece's. So far, two non-elected Italian Prime ministers have been trying hard to introduce structural and institutional reforms to prevent such a crisis. One can only wish the best. But if any outburst in the political process put the process off the track and a debt crisis exploded, such as happened in the neighbor smaller countries a few years ago, it's clear that this time the EU couldn't rescue such a big economy. The reluctance of the IMF to participate in an endless series of rescues to Greece somehow anticipated that risk. An episode of this sort, as undesirable it may be, would certainly be the occasion for the states to regain their own responsibility for fiscal and financial policies, while the EU could also gain more room for developing its own Europe-wide action.

As a consequence of the current financial weakness of the Union, the inequalities in wealth between European states and regions have not diminished as much as could be expected from the existing high levels of integration in trade and in capital and labor mobility. The larger and most developed countries in the center and the North are net contributors to the Union by amounts less than half a percentage point of their GDPs. The relatively small, less developed East European countries are net recipients, including through "structural funds" and "cohesion funds", by amounts up to 3% to 5% of their GDPs. Yet the differences in per capita income between states are in a proportion of about 4:1. Disparities among regions are much higher, up to 12:1, with extremes in Inner London, Brussels and Luxembourg, on one side, and Norwest Bulgaria and Eastern Romania, on the other side. More effective redistribution could only be the consequence of a strengthened and more centralized EU.

To Caesar what's Caesar's

The lesson is, basically, that if the European states wanted the European Union to do more for the European citizens and also do more by themselves, they should accept transferring significant fiscal resources to the Union. The EU should be able to spend more than the current budget of 1% of the Gross European Product. Nowadays, about two-thirds of the EU's budget goes to agriculture subsidies and regional funds, leaving little for other policies able to directly stimulate growth and jobs. Although the Union can also draw from the Central Bank, the Stability Mechanism and the Investment Bank, the total resources available may barely double the EU's strict budget.

Again for comparison, the United States federal government expends more than 20% of GDP. But if we exclude defense and social security, its discretionary power is only about 3% of GDP. Perhaps this could be a provisional target for the EU. It would permit Brussels to expand on some Europe-wide public policies --especially in infrastructures and in research and development, which are both crucial for triggering sustained growth--. And then it would need to interfere less with other policy areas reserved to the states.

The EU's fiscal strength would be the price to pay by the states to reduce EU's overregulation and to regain some of their lost autonomy. In fact, the EU has begun to do part of the job. At the beginning of his mandate, the president of the European Commission, Jean-Claude Juncker, emphasized the EU criteria of subsidiarity, which in French, as he reminded, is taken as synonym of "deregulation". He said to want "an EU that is bigger and more ambitious on big things, and smaller and more modest on small things".

Since 2013, the European Commission has taken more than 200 actions to simplify and reduce regulatory burden and repeal legislation no longer needed. They are mostly in the fields of agriculture, fisheries and environment, the internal market and small and medium enterprises, transport, and migration, visas and citizenship. Also, several dozen existing proposals with low likelihood to become law have been withdrawn or amended.

With the other part of the job were also developed, a less regulatory and fiscally stronger EU would let the states to develop their own policies on the issues on which they would choose to be different, including, in particular, civil law and social spending. The states would be autonomous up to the point of being responsible for their own finances. The states should be able to comply with their own laws and constitutions prescribing balanced budgets without the need to be monitored by the EU institutions. But they should also have the liberty to default and not expect to be rescued by the EU at the expense of the taxpayers of other member-states. Remember that the states of the US were already made responsible for their finances when the federal government was still very weak, by the mid-nineteenth century. So the states of the EU could be now.

In short: it would be possible to acknowledge that the European empire has done much and can do more for us, and let the states and every other level of government do what they can do according to their respective scales of efficiency. To put it again in the imperial context of Roman Judea, we could render to Caesar the things that are Caesar's, and to the states (as well as to the cities and regions) the things that are theirs.

Conversely, the European states may oppose that bargain and may want to keep the bulk of revenue and public spending. But then they shouldn't blame so much the EU for interferences and regulations. In the absence of Brussels fiscal strength, EU's regulations and directives are the only ways by which the Union can try to keep some financial balance in the system, to provide a few European public goods, and to do something for us. A scarcely funded, overregulated European Union will never be a solid federation. Like the US of the early nineteenth century, it will keep maintaining defining characteristics of an empire.

9

The Brussels Consensus

Until not so long ago, the top offices of the European Union were broadly considered to be cul-de-sac posts for politicians trying to pursue an ambitious career. Still in the late 1990s, one of the very few fictional movies set in the EU's headquarters, *The Commissioner*, blatantly reflected that opinion. When a British Cabinet minister was selected by the Prime Minister to be a member of the European Commission, he exclaimed: "Fuck that tombs! Brussels is a political coffin". The media also tended to interpret that this type of appointments were like being booted upstairs, a consolation prize for politicians who had become an embarrassment to their own party in domestic politics.

That's not the situation anymore. The institutional rules most recently adopted in the so-called Treaty of Lisbon, as well as the real functioning of the EU during the recent Great Recession, have enhanced the EU's effectiveness. At the same time, and precisely because the European Union is more powerful than it was some years ago, the EU's institutions are blamed even more than usual for their "democratic deficit".

This evokes, once again, the situation in the United States in the past. Just after the American Civil War, the great nineteenth century English constitutionalist, Walter Bagehot, analyzed the relations between the multiple levels of government in America. He noted that the "efficient" parts, which, in fact, "work and rule" – in Bagehot's words--, were in the nascent Union. He acknowledged, nevertheless, that the Union per se was "new and unattractive" yet. The states were no longer sovereign. But they kept attracting the loyalty of the people that still voluntarily obeyed because they retained "historical and theatrical" elements in their political ceremonies, including parties and elections for recruitment of personnel. The states, deprived of their former sovereignty, but closer to the people, were the "dignified parts" of the new, still emerging system. Given their popular support, the states had become "prerequisites" to run the whole system with sufficient legitimacy.

The situation in Europe nowadays is similar. The Union makes many relevant decisions of government, but state democracies support the selection of most rulers of the Union. From the bottom-up direction, some EU rulers are directly elected, but others are only indirectly selected after state-based democratic elections. The other way around, top-down, increasingly relevant EU legislation on some issues applies directly to all European citizens, but on other issues the Union rules indirectly through state and local governments. Like in America 150 years ago, the European Union is "efficient" because it has significant powers, while the states are "dignified" by historical procedures and theatrical ceremonies. The Union, nevertheless, also tries somewhat to dignify itself by improving and democratizing its own institutions.

The highly efficient, but still new, unattractive and only partly dignified institutions of the European Union work by broad consensus. This model of governance is different from some classical types of governance. On the one side, it is the opposite of adversary politics, as in the typical British system. In the UK, single-party governments formed by either the Conservatives or the Laborites have regularly alternated in government for decades, always based on a minority of popular votes, with only brief periods of coalition governments. The British system is usually praised for effectiveness in decision-making, but at the expense of large popular representation.

On the other side, the EU consensus model is also different from the US model of policy-making by "checks and balances". In the United States, most frequently two different parties control the Presidency and the Congress, and major decisions are feasible only when hard-to-won bipartisan agreements are reached or party discipline is broken. This model is praised for its capability to prevent major decisions based on minority popular support, but it works at the cost of frequent deadlocks and paralysis. The show of the White House and the Congress negotiating until the eleventh hour at the end of the fiscal year to approve the annual budget has become customary.

A super grand coalition

In contrast to the British and the American political models of confrontation and conflict, the European Union works by broad policy consensus. This is fostered by cooperation among multiple political parties and countries in the Parliament and the Council. Let's review the basic functioning of these institutions.

The European Parliament is a directly elected Europe-wide chamber. In practice, it works around a centrist grand coalition formed by the People's party on the center-right, the Socialist party on the center-left, and the intermediate Liberal party. These three parties currently hold together a qualified majority near two-thirds of the Parliament seats, 64%. If the Greens are added on pro-EU matters, they gather together 70% of seats. In spite of being recruited from numerous national parties, the members of each Political Group vote together in the European Parliament around 90-95% of the time.

While the pro-EU parties develop broad cooperation, the opponents to further integration are, in contrast, dispersed and in rivalry. They form the Group of Conservatives and Reformists, which revolves around the British and Polish Conservatives; the United Left–Nordic Green Left Group; the Freedom and Direct Democracy Group, which is formed around the UK Independence Party and the Italian Five Star Movement; and the Europe of Nations and Freedoms Group, which includes the French National Front, the Italian Northern League, the Austrian Freedom Party, and the Dutch Party for Freedom; while the 'Non-Inscrits' collect a bunch of fascist and communist deputies. These gatherings have relatively low internal cohesion and voting discipline, as each party in the Group tends to give priority to national interests.

The other legislative body is the Council of the European Union, also called colloquially the

Council of Ministers or just the Council. It is formed by a representative of each member state at ministerial level. The personal composition of the Council continuously changes, as there is a national election every two months on average, and some governments can frequently be replaced, one after another. It is, thus, assumed that the Council may not focus on temporary partisan orientations of the governments of the moment, but that it rather represents permanent interests of the states on a territorial basis.

This institutional configuration with the Parliament and the Council evokes the typical structure of a federation, where the lower chamber represents the citizens at large and the upper chamber is formed on the basis of territorial units. For example, in federal Germany, the upper chamber or Bundesrat is, analogously to the Council of the EU, formed by representatives of the territorial governments, the laender. Like the states in the EU, the German laender have staggered elections --one about every three months-- and their partisan composition changes with relative frequency.

The Council can make decisions by a majority of 15 of its 28 members comprising at least 65% of the total population of the Union, according to formal rules partially enforced since late 2014 and exclusively from 2017 on. But a minority representing 35% of the population cannot block a decision if it does not include at least four countries. In practice, these rules make the three greatest members, Germany, France and the United Kingdom, unable to block a decision. Even if they could count for near 40% of the total population of the Union, they need additional partners. Also, highly conflictive topics, such as foreign policy, taxation, and social security, still require unanimous agreements. With these rules, it is intended that the Council will not be dominated by any group of member states and that, together with the large members, the interests of small and peripheral ones will also be considered in the decision-making process.

In fact, the Council works by consensus and explicit votes are infrequent. Broad majorities are built through negotiations under the so-called "shadow of the vote", that is by only implicitly checking whether sufficient support for a proposal has been reached. Long deliberations bring about reasoned justifications based on technical knowledge and shared standards. Even when the necessary majority is reached, the Council tends to continue negotiating and make compromises to obtain the support of as many member states as possible.

Then, a decision can be made if no one objects to it at the end of a period set by the chairman (such as a week, for instance). Most members of the Council prefer to avoid registering their dissent by voting against a legislative act or abstaining, as they expect the others will do the same when the differences play in their favor. Raising explicit objections or dissensions to be recorded is usually seen as inappropriate, a violation of "how things are done" in the Council. Between 80% and 90% of the legislative acts are adopted by unanimity without any recorded dissension.

Naturally, consensus is less difficult to attain on those issues in which the level of conflict of interests among countries is low, as we discussed before regarding the stops and goes in the process of European integration. On some relatively conflictive issues, such as agricultural subsidies or certain aspects of the budget, some members of the Council may occasionally adopt visible postures and threat with breaking bargains. The United Kingdom is the country with the highest number of votes against or abstentions registered, particularly on foreign policy decisions.

The consequence of all these formal rules and practical norms is that the Council's agenda focuses on those issues on which broad consensus can be reached, and it sustains significant continuity with previous decisions. Highly controversial issues, thus, tend to be avoided as subjects of EU legislation.

A dual executive

Together with a dual legislative, formed by the Parliament and the Council, the EU has also a dual executive, formed by the Commission and the European Council. The presidents of these two executive bodies usually represent the EU abroad, including, in particular, at the summit meetings of the Group of Seven and the Group of Twenty.

The European Commission is in charge of promoting the general interest of the Union. As a proper executive, the Commission oversees the application of the EU's treaties and law, and it executes the budget. It is also an agenda-setter and initiator of policy and legislation.

The president of the Commission is chosen by the Parliament every five years taking into account the results of the election. During the campaign for the most recent election of Parliament in 2014, for the first time the major European parties presented candidates for president of the Commission. Several public and televised debates were held between Jean-Claude Juncker for the Populars, Martin Schultz for the Socialists, Guy Verhofstadt for the Liberals, José Bové and Ska Keller for the Greens, and Alexis Tsipras for the Left. The candidates spoke mostly in English, although they also delivered speeches in French, German, and other languages. After the Parliament election, the candidate of the most voted party, Juncker, was elected the President of the Commission. He was supported by 61% of members of Parliament and confirmed by 26 of the 28 members of the Council (while the British and Hungarian prime ministers voted against).

The President appoints the commissioners, who are scrutinized closely and submitted to a vote of consent by the Parliament. On the most recent occasion, one of the proposed commissioners, from Slovenia, was turned down by the Parliament and was replaced, as has also happened other three times after recent elections. According to current rules, there could be as few as 20 commissioners chosen by rotation among the 28 member states. Juncker, however, appointed 28 commissioners, one per country, and selected among them only seven vice-presidents with the power to coordinate and filter initiatives from larger areas distributed between the other commissioners. Juncker called the vice-presidents "*petits chefs*" or little bosses who would "instruct the other commissioners." None of the vice-presidents is from any of the three largest countries. The president and three vice-presidents are former prime ministers from rather small countries (Luxembourg, Estonia, Latvia, and Finland). Four of them are from recent Eastern European member states.

The First Vice-President is Frans Timmermans, who is in charge of a portfolio called "Better Regulation, Inter-institutional Relations, the Rule of Law and the Charter of Fundamental Rights." In spite of its elongate name, this office has the opposite intention of shortening and cleaning up the acquis of accumulated legislation and stopping the introduction of new regulations. The other vice-presidencies include the High Representative for Foreign Affairs and Security, Federica Mogherini, and five more in charge of Commission's priorities: Growth, Digital Market, Energy, Budget, and Social Dialogue. The president and the seven vice-presidents are four from the Populars, three from the Socialists, and one from the Liberals, in very close proportion to the parties' representation in Parliament. Likewise, the 28 commissioners are 14 from the Populars, ten from the Socialists, and three from the Liberals, as well as one from the British Conservatives who is in charge of nothing less than "Financial Services and Capital Markets".

In contrast to the old cliché that candidates for top offices in Brussels were unfit local party members or political dinosaurs –to which we refer at the beginning of this chapter-- recent parliamentary hearings have been occasions to evaluate severely their competence and honesty. Although the candidates to commissioners are suggested to the President by the state governments and may have some partisan affiliation, once they are confirmed they swear an oath of independence. As established by the treaties, "the Commission shall be completely independent... and the members of the Commission shall neither seek nor take instructions from any Government or other institutions, body, office or entity".

In fact, the commissioners never allude to their partisan affiliation or ideology in their deliberations. When the discussion deals with some issue particularly related to a country, the commissioner from it does not refer to "my country" but to "the country I know the most". Like most of the other EU institutions, the European Commission makes decisions by consensus and rarely by voting. Ultimately, the Commission is responsible to the Parliament, which may vote a motion of censure to make it resign (as happened in 1999).

The other executive body of the EU is the European Council and its Presidency. As the Commission promotes the general interests of the Union, the European Council reflects the interests of the member states. The European Council is formed by the chief executives of the 28 member states. They are 24 prime ministers and four directly elected executive presidents (from Cyprus, France, Lithuania and Romania, although the directly elected presidents of Finland and Poland have also attended some meetings).

The European Council constitutes the collective presidency of the EU. But it also contains a permanent, full-time individual Presidency, whose holder is in office for up to five years in correspondence to the Parliament and the Commission terms. The current President of the European Council is Donald Tusk, former Prime Minister of Poland. He was selected at a suggestion from the German Prime Minister, Angela Merkel, and accepted by unanimous consent. He reports to the Parliament after each European Council meeting.

Consensus, no partisanship

In a nutshell: the elected European Parliament and the Council representing the states co-legislate on nearly every policy area and they also have significant powers in the process to approve the budget. The centrist grand coalition of Populars, Socialists and Liberals creates consensual proposals in the expectation of being accepted by the Council, which is also formed by representatives of governments mostly led by members of those three parties. They also support the Commission and its president because the three of them all have commissioners inside.

Thus, in contrast to traditional state-based politics, the European Union does not make and implement decisions by partisan competition. The EU avoids drastic alternations in power of political parties with opposite policies, as in the UK. It is also unacquainted with major inter-institutional conflicts produced by different partisan control of different branches of government, as in the US. The EU institutions are based on a double citizenly and territorial representation. They make decisions by broad multiparty central consensus and inter-institutional cooperation.

All in all, it can be said that the claims about the EU's democratic deficit have been somewhat exaggerated. The European Union may still be too "new and unattractive", as the American union was more than one hundred years ago. But it already works and rules.

10

The Rule of Experts

There are many "technocrats" holding high offices and having substantial responsibilities in the European Union. Non-elected experts are frequently criticized and caricatured for being unaccountable and ignoring democratic mandates, and derided as arrogant "Eurocrats". They rule the Central Bank, the Court of Justice, and a high number of specialized agencies. All of them have explicit mandates about what to do; that is, about the goals to pursue and the policies to implement. The assumption supporting their role is that certain policy decisions can be clearly identified by rational analysis and away from partisan fights and short-term electoral demands.

It is still an intriguing question, however, why the rulers of most states have conceded in giving away powers to independent nonelected bodies of experts. Actually the question is as valid at the European level as it is at the state level because the European Union didn't invent "technocratic" rule. The EU, like many other international and global institutions, rather uses some of the criteria, formulas and procedures that were previously developed at the state level. As a matter of fact, professional civil services, self-ruled judiciaries, independent central banks, and self-regulating agencies have always been part of the basic structure of modern states and have proliferated in recent times.

The state rulers began to lose the capability to exert traditional forms of control as the complexity of collective affairs increased and the territorial scope of human exchanges expanded. The actual weakness of politicians at managing some major collective issues has been a source of frustration and disappointment of expectations among voters in modern representative democracies for a long time.

That's why politicians running in elections and holding offices dependent on elections may have been interested in lightening the agenda of issues under their direct responsibility. At some moment, they may have become aware that they were running high risks if they were made politically responsible for certain processes and decisions that develop beyond their reach.

It's a common observation that competitors in near-permanent electoral campaigning tend to skip those issues on which they cannot envisage a clear political advantage over their rivals. The point here is that, nowadays, certain policy issues can be the subject of complex technical decisions alien to traditional types of political controversy. Also, other issues escape the territorial limits of the jurisdiction of the coveted office. Rulers and politicians may prefer to transfer responsibility on those issues to independent technical bodies, whatever domestic or international, rather than to make decisions in the middle of sheer ignorance and to entangle themselves in unsolvable messes.

Focusing on a relative low number of issues in which parties and candidates can present relatively clear and credible stances can help to win elections. Meanwhile, independent expert bodies will do whatever they know to do. Although at different scales and different moments, similar searches of better political survival can, thus, explain why rulers and politicians accept the establishment of independent bodies of experts at the state level and the delegation of state powers to European and international nonelected institutions.

The rulers and top officers of the EU's administration, the European Central Bank and the European Court of Justice, as well as those of the numerous EU specialized agencies, are not recruited on the basis of any previous direct or indirect partisan elections. They are selected with criteria of professional competence, technical expertise, and honesty. They are economists, jurists, engineers and specialists in other fields that can bring about sufficient knowledge, training, and reputation. The assumption is that specialists can identify probable cause-and-effect relationships of complex problems and propose specific policies with predictable consequences. They can also point out salient points for discussion and negotiation and suggest elements to evaluate further results. These virtues are not usually in hand to partisan politicians fighting against each other in search of advantage and triumph. Let's briefly review how the most important independent bodies of the EU work.

Independent Central Bank

The European Central Bank (ECB) has been considered the most independent central bank in the world. This is especially due to the long, non-renewable terms of its managers. But the Bank is not completely independent in setting its agenda and choosing its goals. It's not that it is submitted to any government or another political institution, but that it is bound by an explicit policy mandate for which it is made accountable.

The ECB was created in 1998 to administer the monetary policy of the countries that were going to use the euro. It has the mandate to seek price stability. Specifically, the Bank's monetary policy must aim at "a year-on-year increase in the Harmonized Index of Consumer Prices for the euro area of below 2 percent", which should be "maintained over the medium term". According to the EU's treaties, the Bank must also support the economic policies that can contribute to the achievement of that objective, which in practice has motivated increasing activity in fiscal and financial affairs. Nowadays, the European Central Bank does not only determine key interest rates and the supply of monetary reserves. It also purchases bonds issued by Euro-zone member states and assumes the tasks of supervisor and conflict resolution of the European banking system.

Analogously to the general institutional configuration of the EU, the European Central Bank has a dual structure of internal governance formed by some elements based on the Union at large and others based on the member states: the Executives and the Governors, respectively.

The ECB's Governing Council is composed, on one side, by six Executives appointed by the European Council in consultation with the Parliament (forming the Executive Board). They are selected for a term of eight years "from among persons of recognized standing and professional experience in monetary or banking matters". They meet weekly at the Bank headquarters in Frankfurt am Main, Germany. The current president is Mario Draghi, former governor of the Bank of Italy. He made himself notorious by asserting, in 2012, that "the euro is irreversible" and that the Bank was "ready to do whatever it takes to preserve the euro".

On the other side, the ECB's Governing Council is also composed of 15 of the 19 Governors of the central banks of the countries using the euro. They must also be independent from their governments and hold a minimum term of office of five years. The governors are divided in two groups. The five Euro-zone countries with higher gross domestic product and financial balance (Germany, France, Italy, Spain and the Netherlands) take monthly turns to use four votes, while the other 14 countries take turns to use 11 votes. This distribution of votes is inclusive of all countries, but it's somewhat biased in favor of the larger economies, as the capital of the European Central Bank is also subscribed and held by the national central banks on the basis of the member states' respective shares of gross domestic product and population.

The Bank's Governing Council with both the Executives and the Governors meets twice a month at its headquarters. In spite of the rotation of voting rights, all 19 members attend the meetings. But the Council takes its monetary policy decisions only every six weeks, mostly by consensus after long deliberations. The independence of the Council members is supported by the mandate that "neither the European Central Bank, nor a national central bank, nor any member of their decision-making bodies shall seek or take instructions from [European Union] institutions or bodies, from any government of a member state or from any other body," a norm that the latter institutions must also respect. Like in most EU institutions, voting is a rarity, even more in this case as it's expected that the members' technical expertise must be able to conduce to well-grounded resolutions. The decision-making meeting is followed by a highly-attended press conference and the regular publication of accounts.

Impartial Judiciary

The not well-known European Court of Justice is the oldest institution of the European Union currently existing, as it was created as early as in 1952 at the naissance of the Coal and Steel Community. As it mainly works in French, its most usual acronym tends to be CJUE (for *Cour de justice de l'Union européenne*). From the beginning, the Court was seated in Luxembourg, with the intention to help preserve its independence from the political institutions in Brussels.

The mission of the European Court of Justice is to interpret the EU legislation to make sure it is consistently applied across all the member states. Litigation can be brought before the Court by national governments, national courts, companies, organizations and individual citizens. The Court also acts as the arbiter of competences between the other institutions of the EU. It has the power to dictate sentences that can be enforced either directly or through national courts and governments, including monetary sanctions on EU institutions and member states. The Court of Justice has been more recently supplemented with the General Court, in charge of less complicated cases brought forward by private subjects, especially regarding market competition. The Civil Service Tribunal resolves disputes involving EU staff. Since the establishment of the three courts, approximately 28,000 judgments have been delivered.

Certainly it is not the European Union that invented the idea that judges and magistrates should not be elected by the people, but selected among qualified professionals of law. The independence of the judiciary from the legislative, executive and political process is enshrined as an essential element of the division of powers in free, soft, and balanced governments since the eighteenth century. Only in the United States some judges were traditionally elected in competitive elections. But at some point the formula began to be severely criticized for introducing partisan biases in the administration of justice and most states sooner or later adopted non-elective procedures based on merit.

The European Court of Justice is formed by 28 judges, one from each member state, for renewable six-year terms. In practice, each government nominates a judge who is ratified by the other governments. But the judges must be chosen from persons with high qualifications and competence and "whose independence is beyond doubt". The Court may sit as a full court or in chambers of a few judges. It is helped by nine advocates-general whose job is to present opinions on the cases brought before the Court "publicly and impartially". The current president is Koen Lenaerts, from Belgium.

The Court has been instrumental for the effectiveness of EU regulations and other legal norms. It established the supremacy of EU law over the law of member states already in a couple of sentences on apparently minor cases in the early 1960s. They dealt with the bills of a recently nationalized electric company in Italy and new customs duties in the Netherlands. On those occasions the Court affirmed that, by becoming members of the European Community, "the states have limited their sovereign rights, albeit within limited fields, and have thus created a body of law which binds both their nationals and themselves". Consequently, the EU law cannot be overridden by rules of national law, however the latter are framed and even if they have been introduced after the EU law.

From other cases, the Court has made some basic principles of the EU effective. The free movement of workers is supported by a sentence on a case initially raised by a football player in Belgium aiming to be transferred to a club in a different country. The free movement of capitals was firstly litigated by a travel agent. Some individual rights have also been asserted through jurisprudence, including the establishment of equal pay for men and women at the initiative of a stewardess of a Belgian airline, which was followed by hundreds of female employees across the EU. Other consequential sentences protected the freedom to create companies and market competition and the rights of European citizenship.

Specialized agencies

There are more than 30 specialized EU agencies that deal with a variety of policy issues requiring highly technical solutions. Most of these agencies depend on the European Commission and aim at pooling the technical and specialist expertise available in Europe, away from electoral or partisan processes.

The oldest autonomous agency is the European Investment Bank. It was established immediately after the foundational Treaty of Rome to support infrastructure and development projects. It has co-financed road, rail and communication networks, including, for instance, the Eurotunnel between London and Paris.

A number of decentralized regulatory agencies have also been created, especially since the early 1990s, to deal with economic and social subjects, such as security in maritime, aviation, and railway transports, evaluation and supervision of medicines, or safety of food, among many others. A few also deal with security and judicial cooperation, including Europol, which is a network of national police systems for information and intelligence exchange against terrorism, drug trafficking, money forgery and laundering, and other trans-border crimes. A few executive agencies have also existed for fixed periods, such as the European Research Council, although some of them aim at longer temporal horizons. These agencies have seats all across Europe, from Dublin to Thessaloniki and from Lisbon to Helsinki.

For a long while, the proliferation of EU agencies was the result of case by case decisions, without any plan or vision for their place in the EU institutional structure. By 2008, the European Commission announced a "pause for reflection," which stopped the creation of new agencies and led to evaluations of the existing ones. Three years later some common norms were approved, not only regarding requirements of technical quality but also about their internal organization. Every agency is ruled nowadays by a board formed by one representative from each member-state, who are selected "in light of their knowledge" on the agency's specialty, and by a smaller executive committee. Their members are initially appointed for renewable terms of four years with the wish to foster continuity. All agencies are evaluated for their performance by the Commission every five years.

Efficiency and consensus

There is a close interrelation between the role of independent bodies of experts just reviewed and the working of the EU institutions as it was described in the previous chapter. As we saw before, the emblematic policy consensus of the European Union is promoted and sustained by super grand central coalitions among multiple parties and by cooperation among the main institutions. But the substance of the consensus is greatly due to the work of scientists, technicians and experts, whose policy proposals and solutions are collected and transmitted by independent agencies.

In a broader perspective, one can see how new ideas for efficient policy-making emerge through research institutes, university departments, think tanks, and academic societies that sustain laboratories, organize conferences, publish papers and journals, and promote a variety of transnational contacts, communications and exchanges. Thanks to these networks, policy-makers can accumulate information about public policy decision-making and their implementation, learn from trials and failures, repeat and adapt others' experiences, try to imitate the successful cases, and emulate the best performances.

Outside these processes, it is astonishing what foolish things some state governments can do if they make policy decisions only on the basis of partisan stickiness and permanent confrontation and do not learn from experience and shared knowledge. But when multiple parties or several institutions need to negotiate and agree upon decisions about common policy proposals, as happens in almost every state democratic regime and in the European Union itself, they tend to converge to some focal point previously forged as a technically efficient solution.

That's why the set of diverse institutional mechanisms of the European Union can be efficient and consensual at the same time. They are a combination of directly elected representatives, indirectly appointed high officers, and independent specialists selected for their expertise. Efficient solutions provided by experts are acceptable by multiple parties and institutional consensus because they are efficient, or as long as they are so. And the political consensus is sustainable to the extent that it supports solutions that prove to be efficient. The so-called "Eurocrats" are, thus, one of the crucial components of the institutional structure of the European Union.

11

Nationalist Resistances

During the electoral campaign in Greece in January 2015 that would lead to the victory of the Radical Coalition of the Left, better known by the Greek acronym Syriza, the leader of the far-right National Front in France, Marine Le Pen, declared that she expected Syriza's success and that "we would rejoice in their victory". She declared that "the political divide is not left and right anymore but globalists and patriots", and as in "neither in Greece or Spain there is no equivalent to the National Front" –she said--, "it is the extreme left that takes our place."

In fact, the far-left Syriza chose a far-right, strongly nationalist party, called Independent Greeks, as the partner to form a majority coalition government in Greece. Independent Greeks hold strong anti-immigrant views and archconservative positions on religious, moral and family issues, but it's very close to Syriza in its dismissal of the European Union. The leftist party in Spain, We Can, named Podemos in Spanish, which was initially formed mostly by former Communists, also supports Syriza. Podemos introduced itself as an insurgency of true patriots against the foreign "troika" and the national "caste", taking direct and explicit inspiration on this from the populist Five-Star Movement in Italy. In turn, the Five-Star forms a single Group in the European Parliament with the United Kingdom Independent Party, UKIP, which blames foreigners and immigrants, together with the EU, for all the country's disgraces. After the Greek election, the UKIP leader, Nigel Farage, stated: "I hope Syriza does indeed stick to its guns. Not just because it would hasten the end of the euro, and perhaps prompt a greater debate about a British exit". And so on.

The far-left and the far-right coincide in opposing further integration of the European Union. Most of the parties mentioned, as well as other minor groups in other countries, favor exiting the euro, and some even the Union. Their populism is made of debasing alignments on the left-right or other policy axis and of holding the claim that the main dividing line is between "they and us", between those at the top and those at the bottom. From that angle, the institutions of the EU in Brussels and Frankfurt may look more at the "top" than anything else.

Actually, the main differences between some of those parties do not derive from their leftist or rightist penchants, but precisely from their nationalisms, which may enter them in rivalry and often in opposition of interests. For example, many immigrants in Britain or France come from Greece, Italy or Spain, which place the local nationalist parties on different sides on the issue. All in all, in several countries in Europe, a number of parties with diverse ideological backgrounds make a priority of resisting Europe-wide cooperation and transnational integration by vindicating the sovereignty of the national state.

Europeanist and Atlantist
Social-democrats

Traditionally, the European left opposed resistance to European integration because the left is statist. The foundational and traditional notion of socialism, which some of the new leftist parties want to revive against the moderate orientation of the current Social-democracy, requires a strong state. In a socialist society, the state would be the owner of the means of production, that is, of the industries, banks and services, and the controller of all types of private goods and individuals' lives. A strong state such as the one required by the socialist project is incompatible with depriving the state of substantial commercial, monetary, fiscal and financial policies and entrusting them to the EU.

The adaption of left parties to the development of European integration has followed different rhythms for Social-democrats, Communists, and new Radical Leftists in different countries. The initial European Community treaties in the 1950s were promoted and subscribed to by governments led by Christian-democrats or Social-democrats. Prime Ministers or Foreign Affairs ministers, such as Christian-democrats Konrad Adenauer from Germany, Robert Schuman from France, and Alcide de Gasperi from Italy, closely collaborated with Social-democrats or Laborites, such as Guy Mollet from France, Paul H. Spaak from Belgium, and Sicco Mansholt from the Netherlands, at the first steps of European integration. In four of the six founding member-states of the European Economic Community (EC), there were coalition governments with participation of Social-democratic or Labour parties at the moment of signing the treaty of Rome in 1957.

In other countries, however, including the initial members Germany and Italy, the main left parties were initially opposed or at least reluctant to the European common market. Everybody soon realized that the European project was incompatible with traditional socialist proposals in favor of state-owned enterprises and protection of domestic markets. All across Europe, the left parties were also divided regarding NATO. Generally speaking, those in government were mostly in favor, including the Laborites in the

United Kingdom and the Socialists in France, while anti-American sentiments were still hot among those in opposition.

The German Social-democratic Party (SPD) was a pioneer in dropping Marxism, hostility to capitalism and nationalizations and in abandoning neutralist foreign policy and accepting membership to NATO, as early as in 1959. A few years later, the SPD, led by Willy Brandt and Helmut Schmidt, entered the first of what would be several grand coalition governments with the Christian-democrats. Further on, the Social-democrats were also in government in coalition with the free market-oriented Liberals, as well as with the Greens.

In France, the traditional French Section of the Workers' International (SFIO), which held crystal clear Europeanist and Atlantist positions, had been in government with the Christian-democrats and the Radical-liberals. But it was replaced in the early 1970s by a newly founded Socialist Party, which formed a Union of the Left with the Communists and the Left-Radicals. There were still nationalizations of private companies for ideological motives in France at the beginning of the presidency of Socialist Francois Mitterrand in 1981. It took barely a couple of years, however, for the French Socialist party to abandon such a path. Soon after that, the Socialists initiated the first of several "cohabitations" with the Conservatives. In his second term, Mitterrand appointed Prime Minister Michel Rocard –who was derided as an advocate of "the American left"— to chair a coalition cabinet with the Centrists. The party's allegiance to the EU and NATO was never further discussed. Further on, several leftist alternatives, mostly influenced by Marxist and Communist traditions, were tried, but they didn't achieve governmental status.

In Italy, when the Socialists initially joined as a junior partner a center-left coalition government with the Christian-democrats, in 1963, they advocated a policy of total neutrality and were demanding that Italy withdraw from NATO. Gradually, however, they accepted membership in the EC and NATO, especially under the leadership of Bettino Craxi, who became Prime Minister in a coalition government with the Christian-democrats and other parties in 1983.

The Spanish Socialist party (PSOE) learned the lesson very soon. After losing the first two democratic elections in the late 1970s, the PSOE's leader, Felipe Gonzalez, forced the party to abandon its commitment to Marxism and to adopt pro-market economic policy commitments in 1979. The party won the following election three years later, and it didn't even try to implement nationalizations or similar decisions. Soon thereafter, Spain joined the EC and the Socialist government explicitly embraced NATO membership.

It took longer for the British Labour party to adapt to the EC because, largely as a consequence of its leftist positions, it was in opposition for much longer-than-usual from 1979 on. In its post-war periods of government, the Labour party had nationalized railways and telecommunications, as well as iron, coal, steel, electricity and gas industries. But under the leadership of Tony Blair, the so-called "new Labour" adopted a "third way" between Conservative and traditional Socialist policies. In 1995, the party gave up its pledge to establish "the common ownership of the means of production, distribution and exchange", which, as

"Clause 4", spelled out Labour's aims and values on the back of the party's membership cards. Blair and the Labourites won the election and formed government two years later.

Realist Euro-Communists, Greens and Leftists

All the West European Communist parties condemned the European Communities in the 1950s and 1960s. They blamed the European Common Market for being too much in favor of free market economic policies and against the labor movement, as well as an instrument of NATO, which was in turn condemned as an instrument of American influence in Europe.

However, the re-labeled "Euro-communist" parties of Italy, France, and Spain, as they sought to become credible parties of government by democratic means, accepted the European Community around 1972. Further on along the same decade, the Italian Communist Party (PCI), led by Enrico Berlinguer, declared that it went along with the concept of Italy remaining within the NATO alliance. Gradually, the PCI abandoned Marxism, formed an electoral coalition with former Christian-democrats, as well as a few Greens and Social-democrats, and achieved to lead a coalition government for a year and a half in the late 1990s. After major remodeling that left some small orthodox Communist groups behind, it merged with their coalition partners in a new, vaguely progressive Democratic Party. More recently, the President of the Republic, former Communist Giorgio Napolitano, appointed two successive cabinets of independent experts in order to comply with European Union mandates, until a broad coalition of center-left and center-right parties was formed with the same purpose.

In political contexts such as those just reviewed, which can be defined by the Social-democracy's adoption of mainstream economic policy and the traditional Communists' vanishing or lack of credibility as an alternative, new radical left parties have tried to launch. However, within the European Union, the political space outside and between those two political traditions has proven to be very narrow.

Initially, the German Greens adopted rather radical leftist positions in economic and foreign policies. But internal quarrels in the 1980s led the "realos" to prevail over the "fundis", that is, the realists seeking to participate in government and policy-making over the fundamentalists holding more rigid ideological positions. The Greens were unequivocally anti-Communists, up to the point of merging with the Eastern anti-Communist opposition in a permanent joint candidacy after the reunification of the country. Over time, under the leadership of Daniel Cohn-Bendit and Joschka Fischer, the Greens strongly reinforced their pro-European Union stance and became a regular party able to enter the federal government in coalition with the Social-democrats and several local governments with other partners.

More recent attempts at building political alternatives to the left of the Social-democrats are greatly associated with reactions to changes at European level. It took only six months to the radical left Syriza party in Greece in 2015 to realize that it was unable of effectively opposing the Brussels and Frankfurt consensus. In January, Syriza, largely driven by former Communists, won the election with the promise to revise the previous governments' compliance with the conditions for EU's bailouts. Led by Alexis Tsipras, the far-left party formed a coalition government with the far right nationalists, with whom it shared the anti-EU stances. Yet in July the government called a referendum on the EU deal which, in spite of producing a majority for 'no', moved the government to sign the new agreement. Then the ruling party Syriza split and the prime minister called a snap election for September, which confirmed the far left-far right government coalition and its commitment to comply with the EU.

Rightist nationalists

On the right side of the spectrum, it's nationalist myths in favor of patriotic grandiosity and external isolation that become platforms for anti-European, anti-foreign, and anti-immigrant sentiments. But the nationalist rhetoric of the radical right has substantive connections with some pronouncements of the radical left, including a certain devotion to the state.

For instance, the official program of the National Front of France, which is the largest far-right nationalist party in Europe, blames the European Union as "an instrument to the service of a neoliberal globalizing ideology" that imposes "the markets' dictatorship". According to the party leader's contentions during the campaign for the European Parliament election in 2014, the EU is ruled by "a technocratic elite serving the American and European financial oligarchy". Like the radical left, the National Front wants a "strong state", which would nationalize utilities and banks, erect capital controls, leave the euro, reestablish national control of state borders, and impose the primacy of national law over EU law. Its overarching aim is the restoration of "national sovereignty" against the "Euro-Atlantic logic".

The experiences of anti-EU radical right parties in domestic governments have been scarce, usually short, and mostly disappointing regarding their initial goals. In Italy, the Northern League for the Independence of Padania, led by Umberto Bossi, was in government as a junior partner in coalition with the center-right for a few months in the mid-1990s and for five years at the beginning of the century. The Northern League was accused of anti-immigrant and xenophobic instances. It was also skeptical of further European integration, but to keep its credibility as a governmental party, it acquiesced to the euro and the EU's treaties of Maastricht and Lisbon.

The Freedom Party of Austria, whose leader, Jörg Haider, was accused of sympathies with the Nazis, was a junior partner in a coalition government with the Christian-democrats after the election of 1999. The party had opposed Austria's joining the EU and had tried to resist the introduction of the euro, but it didn't attain any of the two goals. The government coalition was initially subject to sanctions from the European Union, which claimed that it was "legitimizing the extreme right in Europe". The Freedom Party split in 2005, and it has not been accepted again as a governmental partner after the following elections.

In Denmark, the Progress Party had opposed the country's joining the European Union, to no avail, and the Maastricht treaty, which it did help to defeat in referendum against the favorable position of the incumbent government. As the party gradually decreased in voter support, it split in 1995, and it was replaced in parliament by the new Danish People's Party. Both the Progress and the People's parties –together with the radical left— successfully helped to reject the introduction of the euro in a new referendum in 2000. Yet, from that moment on, the so-called "pragmatists" of the Danish People's Party supported from parliament a government of the Liberal and Conservative parties from 2001 to 2011 and a Liberal single-party government from 2015 on, without having ministers in the Cabinet.

A similar formula was tried by the Dutch Party for Freedom, which holds strong anti-Muslim and anti-immigrant stances often indicted as racist and advocates the Netherlands' withdrawal from the EU. The Party for Freedom, led by Geert Wilders, supported a coalition government of Liberals and Christian-democrats from parliament without participating in the Cabinet after the election of 2010. But the experience lasted only two years, as the populists rejected a government's project of annual budget designed to meet EU targets, which was nevertheless approved with alternative support from center-left parties in parliament.

The Sweden Democrats, which reject joining the euro and would want to renegotiate Swedish membership of the European Union, were third in votes and seats in the most recent election. But the center-left coalition government of Social-democrats and Greens succeeded in approving budgets and major legislation by negotiating the support of four centre-right parties, to the exclusion of the far-right and the far-left.

Meanwhile, the Finns party was second in the two most recent elections in Finland. On the first occasion, an alternative broad majority government was formed, including the Conservatives, the Christian-democrats, and the Social-democrats. The second time, in 2015, the Finns were accepted in government in coalition with the Conservatives and the Centrists, only after laboriously negotiating a government program compatible with EU's criteria and demands.

Finally, the French National Front has suffered an almost complete isolation in a different institutional context. In presidentialist France, the direct election of the President is the main occasion for political parties to enter into negotiations and agreements, which are usually reproduced later on in parliament. In 2002, the then leader of the National Front, Jean-Marie Le Pen, was second in votes in the first round of the presidential election and became, thus, one of the two front-runners at the decisive second round, in rivalry with the incumbent Conservative President, Jacques Chirac. From the very moment when this result was announced, on election night, militants from across the entire political spectrum, from Trotskyites to Communists, Greens, Socialists, and Centrists, ran to sustain their adversary Chirac, as he was considered by far a lesser evil than the "facho". At the second round, Le Pen obtained an even lower percentage of votes than at the first round and Chirac was reelected with over 82% support.

On the basis of some survey polls, speculations and bets, some foreign spectators wonder what would happen if the new leader of the National Front, Jean-Marie's politically repudiated daughter, Marine Le Pen, became the most voted candidate in the first round of the upcoming presidential election in 2017. At the risk of making this paragraph obsolete soon, it seems a well-grounded expectation that something very similar to the past election just referred to would likely occur. Anybody-but-Le-Pen seems to be, if not an explicit slogan, at least a straightforward way to choose a candidate for most voters in France.

Adapt or Die

Both radical leftist and radical rightist parties face tragic dilemmas in current Europe. Opposing the standard postulates of market-economy and transatlantic foreign policy requires the adoption of anti-European Union and nationalist positions, which –given the high levels of European integration and the actual strength of the EU-- implies even more insurmountable challenges than in previous decades. The electoral and institutional rules enforced in most countries also ensure that no single party such as any of the populists above reviewed can rule alone. In the best of their prospects, each of them would need to form a parliamentary and governmental coalition with more moderate parties.

If new radical left parties are able to arrive in government, they may again face the quandary of either reversing their campaign slogans, even at the cost of internal quarrels and some breakups – something like what the French, Italian and Spanish Socialists, the British Labourites, the Italian Communists, the German Greens and the Greek leftists did in their times— or suffering a quick governmental and electoral failure, as has happened to all far left alternatives that have been tried.

If radical right parties have new opportunities to enter into negotiations to form a majority government, they will also have to choose either to adapt, becoming a new mainstream party and enter the set of rotating multiparty coalitions –like more or less the Italian Northern League, the Danish People's Party, or the Finns did-- or likely suffering internal crises and splits and being rejected as potential partners by the other parties – as has happened to their Austrian, Dutch, French, and Swedish counterparts.

In the past, dinosaurs could either become birds or extinguish. In Europe today, like in natural evolution, the political species that survive are also the ones most responsive to change.

12

To Brexit or Not to Brexit

The relations between the United Kingdom and the European Union are a little like those in ancient times between Egypt and the Roman Empire, if the reader permits me the irreverence. Like the great Kingdom of Egypt, the United Kingdom had been ahead of its own large Empire in the past, and it has never been fully integrated as just one more member of the new Empire. Likewise, the UK is a highly developed urban economy and by far one of the wealthiest members of the Empire; it is a world center of culture and higher education; and it has an excellent location for trade, financial and cultural exchanges with other areas of the world. Somehow like Egypt regarding the Roman Empire, the UK enjoys a unique institutional status within the European Empire, as it is not submitted to many of the general rules enforced by all the other member units; it has passed through a series of attempts to move in and out the Empire; and it holds sustained maneuvering to preserve its autonomy. So coveted and admired as ancient Egypt once was, the United Kingdom is today, and many Europeans would heavily regret it if it ceased to be a member of the Union.

The point is that a special, unique deal with an outstanding member may be difficult to accommodate in a formal federation. But it is feasible in an imperial-type structure such as that of the European Union because an "empire" permits high flexibility and asymmetry, as has been repeatedly remarked all along this book.

The doubt is whether most British citizens may conform to that. To be sure, British sentiments of alienation from Europe are not new. When Winston Churchill called to construct the United States of Europe in the continent, as we have quoted in chapter 1, the British Empire was still not far from its historical peak and he expected that, therefore, Britain would keep relying upon it and remain outside a newly united Europe. But the quick fading of the British Empire in the aftermath of the Second World War and the parallel beginning of what would become the European Empire moved some British rulers and people to change their approach.

Initially, the UK led the creation of a European association of only free trade, the EFTA in 1960, as an alternative to the European Economic Community which had announced the intention to foster an "ever closer union". But almost immediately, Conservative Prime Minister, Harold Macmillan, probably aware that the world role of the UK was not what it had been, made the first bid for membership to the ECC in 1961. It was followed by similar attempts by Labourite Harold Wilson in 1967 and Conservative Edward Heath in 1970. All of them faced significant resistance, not only from France, a traditional foe, but also within their own parties, while they obtained frank support from the outside Liberals. At last, the United Kingdom became a member of the European Community in 1973, that is, sixteen years after its foundation. Two years later, more than two-thirds of British voters unmistakably approved the membership in a referendum.

The United Kingdom's contributions to the European Empire have been numerous and outstanding. They include: its military force, its liberal approach to free-market exchanges, its global reach through its influence in the United Nations Security Council and the main global institutions, and its crucial support for English as the lingua franca of all Europeans away from the traditional rivalry between French and German. Nothing that could be easily dismissed or forgotten.

Yet, British retreats began to be visible just about ten years after its entry. In the 1980s, Conservative Prime Minister Margaret Thatcher launched her famous exclamation "I want my money back!" She obtained a permanent rebate for Britain on its European Community contributions on the basis that it received less in agricultural subsidies than France and other countries. In the 1990s and 2000s the United Kingdom signed all successive treaties of the European Union, but it didn't join the common currency and stingily picked from new common policies on open borders, interior and justice, and the fiscal compact.

A still major withdrawal was preluded by the British Conservative party's departure from one of the basic European Political Groups for the European consensus, the European People's Party. The Tories went to form a new Group, called Conservatives and Reformists, together with other Euro-skeptical partners in 2009. Further major moves were temporarily postponed during the governmental coalition with the pro-European Liberal-Democrats initiated in 2010. But in 2015 the new single-party Conservative government unleashed a major debate under the prospect of calling a referendum about whether or not to stay in the European Union.

Getting to "Yes"

Prime Minister David Cameron has listed a number of conditions for calling to vote "yes" to stay in the European Union. They present different degrees of availability: some of the conditions are in line with some of the current European Commission's purposes and explicit plans; some of them could be negotiated on the basis of precedent or analogy with previous deals; and some are highly unlikely to be feasible within the existing EU's political configuration, although creative compromises can always be invented. Let us briefly examine the shopping list.

First, the British negotiators ask for scrapping of red tape, for further liberalization of markets, and for transferring some powers back from Brussels to London. On this, they coincide very well with some of the current European Commission's priorities. Its president, Jean-Claude Juncker, committed his Commission "not to interfere from all angles in every detail of people's lives" and launched a number of actions to reduce regulations and repeal unnecessary legislation. The negotiators could celebrate innovative agreements, which could be presented as both Britain's and the EU's success.

Some other British demands may be attained by just using the currently existing institutional mechanisms for decision-making. In particular, the UK can obtain guarantees that its access to common markets in services, which is its most important source of trade and foreign investment, will not be limited. The main concern is, of course, the City, a world financial center whose activity amounts to 10% of the UK's GDP. The British government taxes all banks and funds functioning in London, about half of whose operations are in euros.

The rule to apply for mutual satisfaction on this matter is already in the agreement for the banking union as it was reached in 2013. The European Supervisory Authority of private banks, which involves the European Central Bank, has jurisdiction not only over all the Euro-zone member states but also over the rest of EU members, including Britain. Its aim is to preserve the unity of the European market in financial services, whether in or out the Euro-zone. For that purpose, the Board of Supervisors is subjected to a double-majority rule for decision-making, as was explained in another chapter. This requires that any decision must be supported by both a majority of members of the Euro-zone (19 at the moment) and a majority of the other members (currently nine). It is also established that if, in some unpredictable future, the number of member states using the euro increased and only four or fewer countries remained outside the common currency, at least one vote from the latter would be necessary for the Board to be able to make a majority. Most likely, Britain would have actual veto power on most occasions. Similar arrangements could be confirmed for Britain to continue being an outstanding participant in the European financial and other service markets.

The British government also asks for limiting migrants from EU countries to claim social benefits from the UK's government, such as subsidized housing, aid for children, or unemployment benefits. Some people deride the practice of moving to Britain in the expectation to obtain such advantages as "welfare tourism". If Britain attempted to impose restrictions that would infringe the free movement of people across the EU, they would certainly not be accepted, as this is one of the cardinal four freedoms of the Union. When this claim was first mentioned by the British Prime Minister, the rulers of Eastern European countries promptly expressed their frontal opposition, as it could imply discrimination between European citizens. Actually, some estimates hold that EU immigrants in the UK make, in total, higher contributions in taxes than the costs of public benefits they receive, as most of them are young working men. But persecuting abuse or fraudulent claims or even postponing the access to social welfare benefits after moving in may be a compromise acceptable by some other EU members that also receive numerous migrants, such as France or Germany.

An additional demand to establish longer transition periods for workers from future new EU members to work abroad is insubstantial, as the acceptance of new members have been discarded for a few years, as we mentioned. In any case, any future enlargement and its conditions must be approved by unanimity in the Council, where the UK, as every other member state, has actual veto power.

Finally, some British demands would require changes in the EU treaties, including their ratification by referendum in some countries. Most member states are not ready to consider this type of process because it would be cumbersome, long and politically risky —as it was shown by the failure to ratify the EU Constitution in France in 2005. In any case, any EU treaty change would take much longer to be completed than the period planned for the referendum in the UK.

Specifically, the treaty changes wished by the British government would aim at obtaining the right for a group of national parliaments to veto some EU laws. In fact, the Lisbon Treaty of the EU provides for national parliaments to pronounce on legislative proposals by the European Commission, especially regarding the criterion of subsidiarity. One-third of national parliaments can force the Commission to reconsider a proposal (as they did, for instance, regarding a plan to establish common EU rules on strikes). Two-thirds of national parliaments can directly defeat a proposal. Due to the usual political consistency between the parliamentary majority and the partisan composition of governments in most countries, this demand might be less relevant. As the governments are represented in the Council, they already have the possibility to form blocking minorities on many issues submitted to collective decision.

More complicated is the ambition for Britain to be excluded from the aim of an "ever closer union", which is nothing less than the determination enshrined in the very first line of the founding Treaty of Rome. Yet, some precedent may help to find a legal way. After the Danish voters initially rejected the Maastricht Treaty on European Union, a binding accord was signed by the EU member states and deposited in the United Nations registry for international agreements. Through that accord, one of the states --Denmark at the time and potentially the United Kingdom now-- can choose to opt-out from EU integration in certain areas. Using such an ingenious legal design, the UK would obtain a treaty preserving its powers while the EU wouldn't need to change its treaties.

Separation or divorce

If either the British government or most of the British people didn't find the negotiated agreement with the EU satisfactory, Brexit, that is, the exit of Britain from the European Union could win the referendum. Then the alternatives for the United Kingdom would range from separation to divorce. In other words: from moving out but staying in a little house in the suburbs of Europe to breaking up in search of a new relationship with alternative partners such as the United States, the Commonwealth or the rest of the world.

The first alternative, separation, would imply trying to be more or less like Norway. This Nordic country is not a full member of the European Union because membership was narrowly rejected in referendum twice, always against the positive proposals of the incumbent governments of the moment (in 1972 and 1994). Norway is, nevertheless, a member of the European Economic Area, which includes both the EU and the remains of the EFTA and thus has access to the EU's internal market.

However, in order to participate in the EU market, Norway is submitted to all regulations related to the movement of goods, services, capitals and people, including, for example, regulations on working hours, and product, health and safety standards. For the UK, all the EU directives that had been transformed into national legislation during more than forty years would continue to be binding. Similar to Norway, the UK would also have to contribute to some degree to the EU budget and, as the British government already obtained a rebate many years ago, the difference with the current contribution wouldn't be substantial. The UK wouldn't have vote or participation in EU decision-making. In short, the UK's membership of the Economic Area would retain access to the common markets, but it would imply to apply the EU's regulations without participation.

Alternatively, the United Kingdom could divorce the EU. After completely breaking up with the European Union, it would try to open negotiations for a separate treaty with the EU, for a really special relationship with the United States, or for something similar to the imperial trade preference with the Commonwealth countries that was cancelled when it entered the EC.

Yet, after Brexit there wouldn't be any guarantee that the divorcee Europeans would be ready for a new deal. The EU could afford a "trade war" far better than the UK could. Particularly contentious would be the British access to the EU agriculture markets, which might force the UK to subsidize its agriculture or to raise tariffs against agrarian products from the EU. The European Union also has preferential trade deals with more than 40 countries outside Europe from which the UK would cease to be a partner. In any case, it is likely that European capitals would invest much less in the UK. Some surveys guess that, in contrast, American and Asian capitals could be more attracted by the less regulated British environment. But American or Japanese firms in the automotive, food or computer software industries, for instance, could be discouraged from further investments in Britain if they no longer had duty-free access to the EU market. The City of London would unlikely enjoy open access to Euro-zone financial markets, which would also push some American banks and hedge funds to relocate.

Regarding the option for the United States, Washington has made clear that they do prefer a European Britain, as the "special relationship" between the two countries is interesting particularly because it gives the US a friendly way to interact with the EU. If the UK moved outside the European Economic Area, it would also be left outside bilateral forms of cooperation between the European Union and the United States, including the possible Transatlantic Trade and Investment Partnership.

Finally, the hypothetical revival of deeper links with former members of the British Empire would face barriers such as lack of free trade agreements and currency differences with many of the countries, as well as major territorial and maritime distances. The Conservative Lord Howell of Guildford believed that the latter obstacle would be, nevertheless, overcome because "Commonwealth blood is thicker than international water".

There is no such thing as a free separation or a free divorce. The British economy is highly integrated with the European Union, especially regarding exports, foreign direct investments, and financial services. The predictable economic costs of Brexit are sizable. The hypothetical gains from seeking alternative partners are, as usually happens, remote and uncertain.

There is a big industry of forecast and estimates, led by the Bank of England and the House of Commons Library and formed by numerous think-tanks of different orientations, trying to put numbers to a non-European British economy (See 'Sources' for a list). Conjectures hover around $\pm$ 5% of GDP over 15 years, that is, between 5% net losses and 5% net gains, respectively for extremely pessimistic hypotheses of unfortunate developments and extremely optimistic speculations of good luck. For the most likely, intermediate scenarios, most estimates are within the margins of statistical error. Accordingly, in sane logic, significant risk-propensity should be necessary to bet on such big a move.

The political consequences of Brexit are even less predictable than the economic ones. One that appears highly likely, nevertheless, is Scoxit, that is, the exit of Scotland from the United Kingdom. According to all surveys, by far most Scots want to stay in the European Union. In the 2014 referendum on independence, 55% of Scottish voters chose to stay in the UK. For many of them the promise of further devolution from London may have also helped to make up their minds during the campaign. They may have thought: If we could stay in the EU, even if through the UK, and get a better self-rule, why try a risky adventure in search of the unknown?

Very tellingly, in his very first speech after his reelection in May 2015, David Cameron confirmed both the referendum on the EU and his plan to create in Scotland "the strongest devolved government anywhere in the world". He plans to barter devolution from Brussels to London with devolution from London to Edinburgh.

But if the European referendum failed, many people gauge that Brexit would be the shortest way to Scoxit. Northern Ireland, suddenly separated from the rest of the island by a new border, could also try to relocate within the Republic. For many English, this could be another, unanticipated, possibly final episode of a long, not always well-digested process of dismantling the British Empire. After Brexit, they might find themselves living in Little England, rather than in Great Britain, which may not be a happy end after all.

A Britainless Europe

A European Union without the United Kingdom would be smaller, more German, more Conservative, and weaker in the world. First, the exit of the United Kingdom could trigger a cascade of unilateral demands for less commitment and potential exit by other members of the Union, especially those outside the Euro-zone. The EU would be shaken, its borders would be even less well defined than they are now, and the Union's internal stability, put in jeopardy. At the same time, the relative weight of Germany in the EU, whether in population, economic importance or votes in the Council, would increase. This would likely revive the discussion and the fears about the perils of German hegemony.

That a Europe without Britain would be more Conservative is a paradox, as the departing Britain would have been led by a Conservative government. But, as we discussed, during the most recent period the British Conservative party has not been part of the European super grand coalition that rules in the European Parliament and the other main institutions, as its Conservative component, the European People's Party, does not include the Tories anymore. Without the Euro-skeptical British Conservatives and the anti-European UKIP, the super grand European coalition of Populars, Socialists and Liberals would be consolidated. But after the exit of the British Labourites and Liberal-Democrats, the Populars would increase their influence. Specifically, if the members of the European Parliament elected in the United Kingdom in 2014 left, the European People's Party would encompass up to half the seats in the three-party ruling coalition.

The European Union would also be weaker in the global institutions. The number of permanent members of the EU in the United Nations Security Council would pass from two to one. Without the UK, the remaining EU members of the Boards of the World Bank and the International Monetary Fund would have less influence. It's not clear that the two permanent representatives of the European Council and the European Commission in the Group of Seven and the Group of Twenty would be allowed to keep their seats on behalf of a weakened EU.

The only thing that the Europeans could imagine they would gain without Britons at the table is that the English language would become definitely neutral. All speakers would use English with the same disadvantage, as for all of them it would be an additional language. It would be as bittersweet as eating the estranged wife's well-cooked pastry after her unilateral breakup.

The Unsettled Future of the European Union

The European Union can endure and succeed as an "empire" because empires typically hold uneven levels of formal integration of countries and varied degrees of people's allegiance. Loose borders also create opportunities for expansions and contractions, that is, for changes in the empire membership.

In fact, there has been a kind of trade-off in the EU between external enlargement and internal cohesion. A continuous series of territorial enlargements have prevented more cohesive internal institutionalization. Or perhaps the permanent tendency to expand has been a substitute for the difficult building of a more homogeneous community. That's how the European Empire has remained as much more than a mere common market but much less than a super-state or federation.

The current European system of governance is complex, as it includes multiples levels of government, from local to regional, state and the union. Each level of government deals with different issues, from parks and libraries to trade and finances, just to mention a few examples, depending on the territorial scale at which every policy encompasses all its potential beneficiaries and every public good can be provided more efficiently. None of the government levels has a monopoly on the provision of public goods nor is sovereign to make final decisions on everything. On this, the European Empire is akin to a federation. But, in contrast to typical features of federal states, the most distinctive characteristic of the "imperial" structure of the EU are its asymmetries, that is, the different degrees of integration of countries on different issues and the variety of formulas that link the member states to the center in Brussels.

By approaching the EU as an Empire we have tried to make sense of many quandaries, such as the tensions between the Euro-zone and the other member states, the looseness and porosity of some of its external borders and the frontier conflicts with the neighboring Russian Empire, the economic divisions between Northern, Southern and Eastern Europe, and, in particular, the unease of the UK in Europe and the temptation of Brexit.

In the past, different countries have shown different degrees of willingness to join the transatlantic alliance of defense, the euro, or the agreements on border control, justice and police. In the future, the most likely development is that this type of asymmetries will persist and even augment. A large group of core countries will remain in the Euro-zone, under the jurisdiction of the European Central Bank, the Fiscal Compact, and the banking union, as well in loyalty to the Schengen agreement. Other countries may keep taking benefit from the European single market, but they may also continue to be out of some of other commitments.

The asymmetries can increase as the result of new challenges ahead, such as building a common digital market, long distance transport networks, the energy union, terrorist attacks, external borders control or the homogenization of rules for the labor market or social security systems. Every new issue challenges the European states to integrate public policies that hitherto overlooked. But as many issues involve different degrees of conflict of interests among countries, we should expect that they will achieve different degrees of integration all across Europe.

In fact, the asymmetries already expand beyond the formal membership in the Union, as some nonmembers use the euro or share the agreements on border control or the transatlantic defense even more than some member states. On every issue, some countries make higher contributions than others and participate with varied degrees of activism. The dividing line between full commitment and specific associations is thin and contains several shades of grey. In the future, voluntary associations, rather than homogeneous territorial governance, may loosen up the very definition of membership.

In the last chapter, we compared different possible formulas of relationship after a possible exit from the Union with a separation and a divorce. More generally, the same type of simile can be used to describe the variety of allegiances of different countries to the common policies of the European Union. The whole set of varied networks and allegiances can evoke complex family relationships, which are composed of the nuclear family and several connections with first-, second- and third-degree relatives. The actual interactions are partly determined by blood, but affinities, exchanges, and animadversions can also derive from voluntary choices.

Likewise, some countries can behave like either siblings, first-cousins or second-cousins with the European Union, shift between closer and looser relationships with it, choose opt-ins and opt-outs, and enter or leave the Union with different prenups and settlement packages. The Union can also introduce reallocations of powers between the different jurisdiction levels. And the changes may not always be in the same direction, whether towards higher unity or in favor of more diversity.

The European Union is comparable to past imperial experiences also because its institutions are a mix of directly elected representatives, indirectly selected high executives, and appointed independent experts. Like in classical empires, typical institutional formulas and processes in the EU include overlapping authorities, weighted votes to different territorial units, centralizing pulls and nationalist resistances, and broad negotiations and compromises.

Some arrangements of the EU can be transitory. Actually, the history of the Union is a succession of non-anticipated treaties that, one after another, innovate and reform previous agreements and rules. Against some initial plans, the EU has not been built step by step, but with numerous stops and goes. Some people may want to see the current empire as a stalled stage of building a homogeneous political community where centralizing rulers are unable to complete the process. But the image of "incompleteness" of the European Empire is only an optical effect provoked by the mirage of a United States of Europe. The empire may not be an intermediate stage between a set of sovereign states and a united federation. The asymmetries and the diversity of the European Union are not necessarily transitional. With the current configuration and in the foreseeable future, they are bound to endure.

ACKNOWLEDGMENTS

This book was awarded the 2016 Essay Prize of the Fondation Europa Cultural, headquartered in Geneva, Switzerland, which the author happily acknowledges.

The book was written thanks to collaborations with several units of Georgetown University (BMW Center for German and European Studies, Department of Government, School of Foreign Service and McDonough School of Business), the Council for European Studies, the Delegation of the European Union to the United States, the National Intelligence Council, the Eurasia Group, the Peterson Institute for International Economics, the University of Pittsburgh's European Union Center of Excellence & European Studies Center, the Brookings Institution's Center on the United States and Europe, the Center for Strategic and International Studies' Europe Program, the Conference on

Liberalism in the 21st Century at Oxford University, the University of Bristol's Chair in Comparative European Politics, K&L Gates, the European Council on Foreign Relations, Eurointelligence, *El Pais*, *Fair Observer*, and *Financial Times*.

I acknowledge information, ideas and suggestions from encounters and exchanges with Joaquín Almunia, Jeff Anderson, Catherine Ashton, Robert Woodthorpe Browne, Elizabeth Covington, Antonio De Lecea, Juan Díez Medrano, Robert Fishman, Stella Ghervas, Magali Gravier, Stefan Grobe, Ignasi Guardans, Randall Henning, Fiona Hill, Simon Hug, Roger Kubarych, Mark Leonard, Richard Little, Helen Margetts, Juli Minoves-Triquell, Richard Moore, Noel Parker, Wolfango Piccoli, Georges Pineau, Aviel Roshwald, Michael Rowe, Javier Solana, Enrico Spolaore, Rein Taagepera, Peter Turchin, Angel Ubide, João Vale de Almeida, Guy Verhofstadt, Nicolas Veron, Xavier Vidal-Folch, Graham Watson, Martin Wolf, and Jan Zielonka.

SOURCES

Many data and documents are available at the official website of the European Union: www.europa.eu.

Sources for other data and quotations follow.

1. Is the European Union an Empire?

Jose Manuel Durão Barroso's speech is available at https://www.youtube.com/watch?v=-I8M1T-GgRU

The first time I heard of the European Union as an empire was in Washington in 1998 in conversation with the historian Enric Ucelay-Da Cal, who wrote "the construction of the European Economic Community could seriously be taken as the reconstitution of an empire in compensation for colonial loss by the major Western European states" (in 'Nationalisms in Spain. Some

Interpretative Proposals', University of East Anglia 1999; he had anticipated the idea in 'Europa: cronica de un imperialismo', in *Enciclopedia de Europa* 1995). Further works on the European Union as an empire include, in chronological order of publication: Josep M. Colomer, *Grandes imperios, pequenas naciones*, Anagrama 2006; and *Great Empires, Small Nations*, Routledge 2007; Jan Zielonka, *Europe as Empire: The Nature of the Enlarged European Union*, Oxford University Press 2007; Magali Gravier and Noel Parker eds., 'Imperial power and the organization of space in Europe and North America', special issue of the *Journal of Political Power* (with contributions by the editors Gravier and Parker, and by Edward Ashbee, Josep M. Colomer, Peter Halden, Stefan Heumann, Uffe Østergård, Jeppe Strandsbjerg, and Jan Zielonka), 4:3, 2011; Gary Marks, 'Europe and Its Empires: From Rome to the European Union', *Journal of Common Market Studies*, 50, 1: 1-20, 2012; Magali Gravier, 'Stable Core, Shifting Periphery? The European Union as an Emerging Inwards-Outwards Governing Empire', WP 39, European University Institute-RSCAS, 2015.

More generally on empires as a form of polity, S.N. Eisenstadt, *The Political System of Empires*, The Free Press 1963; Maurice Duverger ed., *Le concept d'empire*, Presses Universitaires de France, 1980; Michael W. Doyle, *Empires*, Cornell University Press, 1986; George Von der Muhll, 'Ancient Empires, Modern States, and the Study of Government', *Annual Review of Political Science*, 6, 2003; Peter Turchin, *War and Peace and War: The Rise and Fall of Empires*, Plume 2006; Jennifer Pitts, 'Political Theory of Empire and Imperialism', *Annual Review of Political Science*, 13: 211-235, 2010.

Henry Kissinger, *World Order*, Penguin 2014: 92.

Jean Monnet, 'A Ferment of Change', *Journal of Common Market Studies*, 1, 1: 203-211, 1962. Winston Churchill's speech at Zurich University, 19 September 1946. These and other documents are also compiled in *Giving Shape to an Idea of Europe*, Anthem Press/Council of the European Union 2009; and Brent F. Nelsen and Alexander Stubb eds., *The European Union, Readings on the Theory and Practice of European Integration*, Lynne Rienner, 2014.

2. Goodbye, Sovereignty

For multilevel governance, Liesbet Hooghe and Gary Marks, *Multi-Level Governance and European Integration*, Rowman and Littlefield 2001.

Jan-Claude Juncker's words, in 'The Quest for Prosperity', *The Economist*, 17 March 2007. For electoral results, Josep M. Colomer, 'Firing the Coach: How Governments Are Losing Elections in Europe', *Democracy & Society*, 10:1, 1-6, 2012.

3. The German Core

Thomas Mann, Lecture at the University of Hamburg, 1953. Ulrich Beck, *German Europe* (2012), Polity 2013.

4. The Wild East

European Agency for the Management of Operational Cooperation at the External Borders of the Member States of the European Union (Frontex): http://frontex.europa.eu

On the Bulgarian border: 'Border of Death', *Vagabond*, 19 February 2015; Rick Lyman, 'Bulgaria Puts Up a New Wall, but This One Keeps People Out', *New York Times*, 20 April 2015.

Donald Tusk, 'Lunch with the FT: Donald Tusk', *Financial Times*, 28 November 2014.
Bill Clinton, *My Life*, A. Knopf 2004: 750, 758.
Boris N. Yeltsin, *The Struggle for Russia*, Times Books 1994: 136.

On borders and frontiers in Europe, also: Robert Cooper, *The Breaking of Nations*, Atlantic 2003; Josep M. Colomer, *Europe, Like America: The challenges of building a continental federation*, laCaixa, 2010; John J. Mearsheimer, 'Why the Ukraine Crisis Is the West's Fault', *Foreign Affairs*, September/October 2014.

5. What Europe Has Done for You

The Federalist Manifesto by Altiero Spinelli and Ernesto Rossi, in www.altierospinelli.org.

Robert Schuman's Declaration on 9 May 1950.

The seminal work on functionalism was Ernst B. Haas, *The Uniting of Europe: Political, Social, and Economic Forces, 1950-1957*, Stanford University Press, 1958. For critical discussion, Andrew Moravcsik, *The Choice for Europe: Social Purpose and State Power from Messina to Maastricht*, Cornell University Press, 1998; Enrico Spolaore, 'What is European Integration Really About? A Political Guide for Economists', *Journal of Economic Perspectives*, 27:3, 125-144, 2013.

7. Too Much Regulation, Too Little Budget

Regarding legislation of the EU, during the most recent period with available data, the year 2014, it can be counted that the European Union approved 1,721 legislative acts. Specifically, the

European Parliament and the Council approved 58 regulations directly binding all European citizens and 37 directives to be transformed into national law or administrative acts by the member states, the Council approved 47 regulations and 2 directives, and the Commission enacted 864 regulations and 14 directives. The number of decisions of all EU institutions binding only specific groups of companies amounted to 699 in 2014.

For the sake of comparison, during the same period, the United States Congress approved 72 laws directly binding all US citizens while about 2,500 to 4,000 administrative rules are published per year. During the annual season 2013-2014, in the United Kingdom the Parliament approved 36 laws while the delegated legislation to the ministries, mostly in the form of Statutory Instruments, rarely falls below 3,000 per year. In France, for the same annual season the National Assembly approved 40 laws while a few thousand codes and ordinances were also enacted. For the UK and France, these numbers include the legislation directly derived from EU directives.

Of course, over time the cumulative numbers skyrocket. The total number of legislative acts by the EU institutions during the last two decades amounts to about 12,000 regulations and 2,000 directives. Yet every country with longer legislative history than the EU enforces much higher amounts of accumulated legislation. For the oldest ones, such as the US, the UK, France or Spain, nobody has been able to complete the counting through thousands and thousands of pages of statutes and codes.

Sources:

For the EU: Eur-Lex at
http://eur-lex.europa.eu/statistics/2014/legislative-acts-statistics.html
and EU-ABC at http://en.euabc.com.

For the US:
Congress at
https://www.congress.gov,
National Archives at
http://www.archives.gov/legislative,

and Library of Congress at
http://blogs.loc.gov/law/2013/03/frequent-
reference-question-how-many-federal-laws-are-
there.

For the UK: Parliament at
http://www.parliament.uk,
and Hansard Society at
http://www.hansardsociety.org.uk.

For France: National Assembly at
www.assemblee-nationale.fr.

Randall Henning and Martin Kessler, 'Fiscal
Federalism: U.S. History for Architects of
Europe's Fiscal Union', Peterson Institute for
International Economics, January 2012; and
Henning, 'California's Lesson for the Euro', *The
Prospect*, June 20, 2012.

8 A Faustian Bargain

Data for fiscal balances from 'EU expenditure &
revenue 2007-2013', eurostat.

Varoufakis' confession in 'Exclusive: Yanis Varoufakis opens up about his five-month battle to save Greece', *New Statesman*, 13 July 2015.

9. The Brussels Consensus

Walter Bagehot, *The English Constitution*, 1867.

For European institutions: Josep M. Colomer ed., *Comparative European Politics*, Routledge 2008; Peter Norman, *The Accidental Constitution. The Making of Europe's Constitutional Treaty*, Brussels: EuroComment 2005.

For the Parliament: Vote Watch Europe: http://www.votewatch.eu.

For the Commission: Jean-Claude Juncker, 'A New Start for Europe: My Agenda for Jobs, Growth, Fairness and Democratic Change', Strasbourg, 15 July 2014; 'Setting Europe in Motion: President-elect Juncker's Main Messages

from his Speech Before the European Parliament',
Strasbourg, 22 October 2014.

For the European Council:
htpp://www.consilium.europa.eu

11. Nationalist Resistances

Abel Mestre, 'Marine Le Pen: Oui, nous espérons
la victoire de Syriza', *Le Monde*, 20 January 2015,
'Régionales 2015: pour Marine Le Pen, «le clivage
politique sépare désormais mondialistes et
patriotes»', *Le Monde*, 13 December 2015; *Notre
Projet. Programme Politique du Front National*, available
at http://www.frontnational.com,_2015. Pablo
Iglesias, 'Understanding Podemos', *New Left
Review*, 93, May/June 2015.

12. To Brexit or Not to Brexit

Reports about the foreseeable economic
consequences of Brexit include: Vaughne Miller,
Leaving the EU, House of Commons, 1 July 2013;

Gianmarco Ottaviano, Joao Paulo Pessoa, and Thomas Sampson, *The Costs and Benefits of Leaving the EU*, 13 May 2014, and *Brexit or Fixit? The Trade and Welfare Effects of Leaving the European Union*, Centre for Economic Performance, March 2015; John Sprinford and Simon Tilford, *The Great British Trade-off. The impact of leaving the EU on the UK's trade and investment*, Centre for European Reform, January 2014, and *The Economic Consequences of Leaving the EU*, Centre for European Reform, June 2014; Ralph Buckle, Tim Hewish, John C. Hulsman, Iain Mansfield, and Robert Oulds, *Brexit: Directions for Britain Outside the EU*, Institute of Economic Affairs, 2015; *What If…? The Consequences, Challenges and Opportunities Facing Britain Outside EU*, Open Europe, March 2015; *Brexit: Potential Economic Consequences if the UK Exits the EU*, Bertelsmann Stiftung, May 2015.

BIBLIOGRAPHY

Bagehot, Walter. 1867. *The English Constitution.*

Beck, Ulrich. 2013. *German Europe.* London: Polity.

Bertelsmann Stiftung. 2015. *Brexit: Potential Economic Consequences if the UK Exits the EU.* Gütersloh.

Buckle, Ralph, Tim Hewish, John C. Hulsman, Iain Mansfield, and Robert Oulds. 2015. *Brexit: Directions for Britain Outside the EU.* London: Institute of Economic Affairs.

Centre for Economic Performance. 2015. *Brexit or Fixit? The Trade and Welfare Effects of Leaving the European Union.* London: CEP.

Centre for European Reform.2014..*The Economic Consequences of Leaving the EU.* London: CER.

Clinton, Bill. 2004. *My Life.* New York: A. Knopf.

Colomer, Josep M. 2006. *Grandes imperios, pequenas naciones.* Barcelona: Anagrama.

Colomer, Josep M. 2007. *Great Empires, Small Nations.* London: Routledge.

Colomer, Josep M. ed. 2008. *Comparative European Politics.* London: Routledge.

Colomer, Josep M. 2010. *Europe, Like America: The challenges of building a continental federation.* Barcelona: laCaixa.

Colomer, Josep M. 2010. *The Science of Politics.* New York: Oxford University Press.

Colomer, Josep M. 2012. 'Firing the Coach: How Governments Are Losing Elections in Europe', *Democracy & Society*, 10:1, 1-6.

Cooper, Robert. 2003. *The Breaking of Nations.* London: Atlantic.

Council of the European Union. 2009. *Giving Shape to an Idea of Europe.* London: Anthem Press.

Doyle, Michael W. 1986. *Empires.* Ithaca, NY: Cornell University Press.

Duverger, Maurice ed. 1980. *.Le concept d'empire.* Paris : Presses Universitaires de France.

Eisenstadt, S.N. 1963. *The Political System of Empires.* New York: The Free Press.

Gravier, Magali. 2015. 'Stable Core, Shifting Periphery? The European Union as an Emerging Inwards-Outwards Governing Empire', Working Paper 39. Florence: European University Institute-RSCAS.

Gravier, Magali, and Noel Parker eds. 2011. 'Imperial power and the organization of space in Europe and North America', special issue, *Journal of Political Power*, 4: 3.

Haas, Ernst B. 1958. *The Uniting of Europe: Political, Social, and Economic Forces, 1950-1957*. Stanford, CA: Stanford University Press.

Henning, Randall. 2012. 'California's Lesson for the Euro', *The Prospect*, June 20.

Henning, Randall, and Martin Kessler. 2012 'Fiscal Federalism: U.S. History for Architects of Europe's Fiscal Union', *Peterson Institute for International Economics*, January.

Hooghe, Liesbet, and Gary Marks. 2001. *Multi-Level Governance and European Integration*. New York: Rowman and Littlefield.

Juncker, Jean-Claude. 2014. 'A New Start for Europe: My Agenda for Jobs, Growth, Fairness and Democratic Change'. Strasbourg: European Commission.

Juncker, Jean-Claude. 2014. 'Setting Europe in Motion: President-elect Juncker's Main Messages from his Speech Before the European Parliament'. Strasbourg: European Commission.

Kissinger, Henry. 2014. *World Order*. London: Penguin.

Marks, Gary. 2012. 'Europe and Its Empires: From Rome to the European Union', *Journal of Common Market Studies*, 50, 1: 1-20.

Mearsheimer, John J. 2014. 'Why the Ukraine Crisis Is the West's Fault', *Foreign Affairs*, September/October.

Miller, Vaughne. 2013. *Leaving the EU*. London: House of Commons.

Monnet, Jean. 1962. 'A Ferment of Change', *Journal of Common Market Studies*, 1, 1: 203-211.

Moravcsik, Andrew. 1998. *The Choice for Europe: Social Purpose and State Power from Messina to Maastricht*. Ithaca, NY: Cornell University Press.

Nelsen, Brent F., and Alexander Stubb eds. 2014. *The European Union, Readings on the Theory and Practice of European Integration*. Boulder, Co.: Lynne Rienner.

Norman, Peter. 2005. *The Accidental Constitution. The Making of Europe's Constitutional Treaty*. Brussels: EuroComment.

Open Europe. 2015. *What If...? The Consequences, Challenges and Opportunities Facing Britain Outside EU*. London: Open Europe.

Ottaviano, Gianmarco, Joao Paulo Pessoa, and Thomas Sampson. 2014. *The Costs and Benefits of Leaving the EU*. London: Centre for Economic Performance.

Pitts, Jennifer. 2010. 'Political Theory of Empire and Imperialism', *Annual Review of Political Science*, 13: 211-235.

Spolaore, Enrico. 2013. 'What is European Integration Really About? A Political Guide for Economists', *Journal of Economic Perspectives*, 27:3, 125-144.

Sprinford, John, and Simon Tilford. 2014. *The Great British Trade-off. The impact of leaving the EU on the UK's trade and investment*. London: Centre for European Reform.

Turchin, Peter. 2006. *War and Peace and War: The Rise and Fall of Empires*. New York: Plume.

Ucelay-Da Cal, Enric. 1995. 'Europa: cronica de un imperialismo', in Ramon Castello ed. *Enciclopedia de Europa, vol. 1. Europa y el mundo*. Barcelona: Planeta, 16-27.

Ucelay-Da Cal, Enric. 1999. 'Nationalism in Spain. Some Interpretative Proposals', in Isabel Burdiel and James Casey eds., *Identities: Nations,*

Provinces and Regions, 1550-1900. University of East Anglia.

Von der Muhll, George. 2003. 'Ancient Empires, Modern States, and the Study of Government', *Annual Review of Political Science*, 6.

Yeltsin, Boris N. 1994. *The Struggle for Russia.* New York: Times Books.

Zielonka, Jan. 2007. *Europe as Empire: The Nature of the Enlarged European Union.* Oxford: Oxford University Press.

Websites:

EU-ABC: http://en.euabc.com
Eur-Lex:
http://eur-lex.europa.eu/statistics/
2014/legislative-acts-statistics.html
European Council:
http://www.consilium.europa.eu
European Union: http://www.europa.eu
Eurostat. http://ec.europa.eu/eurostat
Frontex: http://frontex.europa.eu
Vote Watch Europe: http://www.votewatch.eu

UK Parliament at
 http://www.parliament.uk
Hansard Society at
http://www.hansardsociety.org.uk
Financial Times: http://www.ft.com
The Economist: http://www.economist.com
The Guardian: http://www.theguardian.com
New Left Review: http://newleftreview.org

US Congress: https://www.congress.gov
US Library of Congress: http://blogs.loc.gov
US National Archives:
http://www.archives.gov/legislative
New York Times: http://www.nytimes.com

France National Assembly:
http://www.assemblee-nationale.fr
Front National: http://www.frontnational.com
Le Monde: http://www.lemonde.fr

Altiero Spinelli: http://www.altierospinelli.org
El Pais: http://www.elpais.com
YouTube: http://www.youtube.com